A TREASURY OF

AMERICAN BOTTLES

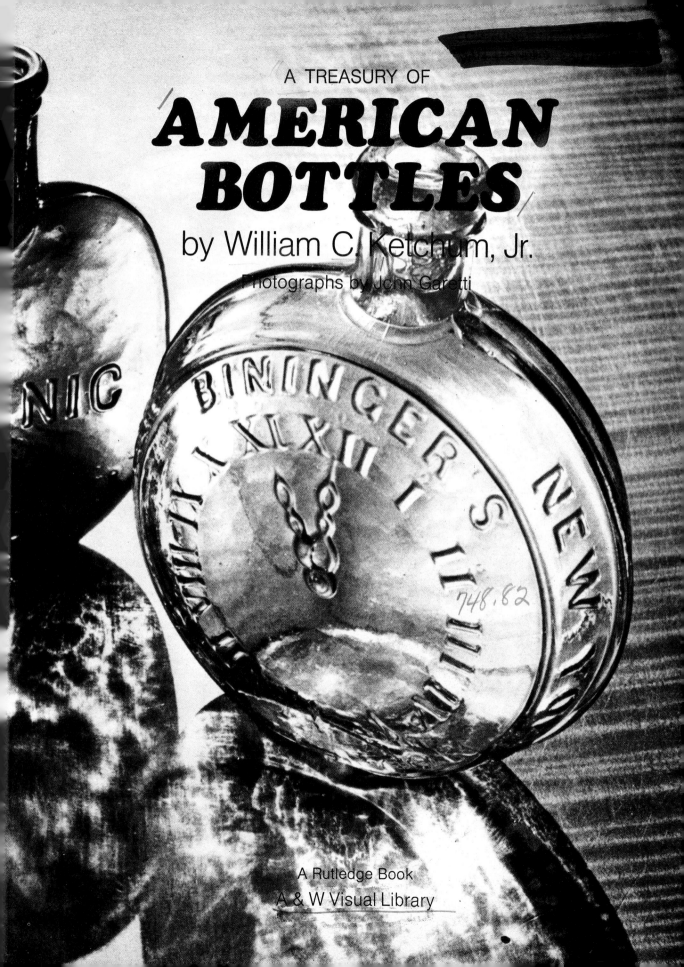

A TREASURY OF

AMERICAN BOTTLES

by William C. Ketchum, Jr.

Photographs by John Garetti

A Rutledge Book

A & W Visual Library

Contents

Introduction

Within the relatively short span of fifteen years, collecting early American bottles and flasks has grown from a hobby enjoyed by the dedicated few to one followed by people of all ages and pursuits. If any inanimate object can be said to have charisma, it must indeed be the old bottle. Collectors of these desirable pieces of glass currently number well in the hundreds of thousands, with converts to the hobby appearing daily.

The urge or instinct to gather items together runs through all the animal kingdom. Ravens do it; chimpanzees do it; and humans certainly do it. Ask the average collector why he collects what he does, and he will probably say it's because he finds it amusing or interesting, relaxing or exciting. "But," asks the uninitiated, "why collect such lowly things as bottles made from so common a material as glass?" The answer to this was nicely summed up by the renowned collector of early American glass and historical flasks, Crawford Wettlaufer, when he said about his collecting that he sought "the extraordinary in the ordinary." In old glass bottles can be found the qualities that make them desirable today.

Firstly, an old bottle has age. Most of the bottles sought today were made before the introduction of the automatic bottle-making machine. Rarity and excellence of condition, attributes important in all realms of collecting, are no less so here. The law of supply and demand decrees that rarity creates desirability and value, as long as the rare bottle is desired by a sufficient number of collectors. That number is growing.

Bottles can be found in a myriad of shapes and colors, as the reader of this book will discover. An old square perfume bottle has nowhere near the appeal of such a bottle in the shape of a child or other figure. Collector interest increases a hundredfold at the chance to possess a historical flask in vibrant blue or claret if that particular flask is usually found in aquamarine.

The more crudely a bottle was made, the greater is its general appeal. A collector of fine porcelains may not understand this. Beauty lies not in any objective quality but in the personal response the quality may evoke. Utilitarian objects made by human hands possess an individuality, an aura, a folk-art quality that machine-made articles cannot match. No two man-made items are exactly alike. A glassblower making the same object gives it variations each time he makes it—a little more glass here, a little less there, a sheared lip on one bottle and an applied flange on the next. A crudely made, pontil-marked medicine bottle can speak volumes to us collectors, while its perfectly formed machine-made cousin produces only silence.

From words embossed in the glass, we can track down information about a person, a place, or a time. This discovery of historical detail gives collectors a delicious feeling of association with where the bottle might have been and what people were like who used its contents. While it isn't very likely that a calabash bottle with an embossed bust of the famous Swedish singer Jenny Lind was actually used by her, collectors can certainly imagine! We recreate the history of our bottles and vicariously live their life stories.

With information currently available, we know fairly well when any bottle was in production. To examine a fine Lafayette historical flask and know it was made in

Amber Huckleberry bottle for preserving wild berries. (Courtesy Burton Spiller)

1824–1825, during the general's final visit to America, is to inspire the present and keep young the face of the past. An old medicine bottle tantalizingly embossed "Swift's Syphilitic Specific," or one marked "Dr. Kilmer's Wild Indian Female Cancer Secret," evokes vivid associations of what the time was like when such bottled therapy could be purchased. For some, these are not merely bottles, but symbols of a historic period. There is a degree of romance about a past time of which we were not any part; there is romance in old bottles.

If the characteristics of age, rarity, condition, crudeness, shape, color, and association are important to bottle collectors, what kinds

of collections are being built today? Simply accumulating any old bottle that comes along is not truly collecting. According to the dictionary, a collection implies some order, arrangement, or unity of effort. Nothing is really a collection that does not partake of these elements. Many collectors are specializing in one field of the hobby. Some collect only medicine bottles, while others may specialize further and collect a specific kind of medicine bottle, such as those embossed "Balsam," "Cure," or "Bitters." Others seek only beer bottles, or fruit jars, or drugstore bottles. Some limit their collecting to bottles of only one color, while still others strive for the best specimens of items in every category. The true collector uses order and reason in assembling his collection to build of its various parts a unified whole. Such a bottle collection is not casual but is made with thought and effort, often in competition with others. Building a distinctive collection is largely a matter of ingenuity, ability, and occasionally luck. It also is a game filled with suspense and adventure, both of which bottle collectors vastly enjoy. Their lives are in many ways richer for their collecting.

When an individual has something in common with other individuals, what can be more pleasurable than sharing this common interest? This desire to share has prompted the formation of many bottle clubs presently active in all states. One typical club is the Genesee Valley Bottle Collectors Association, which serves collectors in the Rochester, New York, area. The club was founded for the purpose of discussing and enjoying all kinds of information relative to the hobby, a purpose achieved by monthly meetings centering around bottles and related topics. Beginning with a mere dozen interested people, this club has grown to over two hundred family memberships. A monthly newsletter keeps

Opposite top: Lithographed tin serving tray for Green River Whiskey. *Opposite bottom:* Lithographed tin advertising sign for Lash's Bitters. *Below:* Barrel-shaped bitters bottles. (All, courtesy Burton Spiller)

the members who cannot attend all the meetings up-to-date.

Some club members are strictly diggers; that is, they seek abandoned dumps and old homesites and with pick and shovel dig up bottles former generations threw away. Who knows what jewel may be unearthed? Other members are chiefly buyers, using the "silver pick" to add to their collections. Many do both, and everyone swaps. Trading one's duplicates is a common occurrence at every meeting.

The highlight of each year is the club's annual show and sale. Here members display their treasures and compete for trophies and other awards in a formally arranged judging system. An important part of each show are the dealers who offer their wares for sale. The majority of dealers also collect. Nothing is more pleasing than to be able to say after a bottle show, "I really had a great time—I spent more than I sold!"

To have something and not share the joy of it with others is as personally unfulfilling as it is unrewarding. Objects that can touch a person in any way are both nourishing to the inner self and psychologically elevating. Through the club, members can appreciate and find pleasure in each other's discoveries. Differences in sex, occupation, and education fade away when bottle collectors meet. Friendships made here are frequently close.

In the pages that follow, the noncollector will come to understand why these things can so turn people on. The avid collector will become even more enthusiastic as he gains deeper insights into his field, along with an increased sense of pride in it. Bill Ketchum's text admirably summarizes every phase of the hobby, from his discussion of the men who developed the American glass industry and bottle manufacturing methods, through his chapters on individual collecting

categories: pictorial and historical whiskey flasks; glistening and jewellike pontil-marked medicine bottles; graceful barber bottles; charming perfumes and colognes; colorful fire grenade bottles; practical fruit jars; elegant figurals; and the several other types that are the heart and soul of the bottle world.

No other book on the subject has photographs to match the quality of John Garetti's. No other bottle book can boast the visual feast of so many magnificent color photos. The effect of seeing a fine old bottle in black and white followed by a color shot of the same one is akin to seeing *Gone With the Wind* first in black and white and then once more in color. Your concept of its intrinsic beauty is enormously enhanced.

Mr. Ketchum's text and Mr. Garetti's photos consummately highlight the esthetic perception of old bottles. The make-up of some collectors is such that beauty of form and color is most important to them. For others, technical and historical background and related significance mean the most. The line that divides collecting bottles for the sake of esthetic pleasure from collecting to satisfy mental inquisitiveness often determines the special emphasis each collector will place on his possessions. To respond intelligently to either basic interest, some degree of critical evaluation must be developed. The great delight of Mr. Ketchum's book is the fine way he helps his readers to accomplish this goal.

A Treasury of American Bottles should become part of every collector's library. It will be read and admired again and again. To seek "the extraordinary in the ordinary"— Bill Ketchum shows us how to do just that!

DR. BURTON SPILLER
Genesee Valley Bottle Collectors Association
Rochester, New York
June, 1974

Clear glass figural cologne bottle in form of a crying baby. (Courtesy Burton Spiller)

1
Early Glassmaking in America

Above: Milk glass barber bottle with clear glass-covered lithographic insert of woman's face. (Courtesy Burton Spiller) *Opposite:* Cobalt barber bottle with white painted decoration similar to work done by Mary Gregory, a decorator at the Sandwich Glass Works. (Courtesy Emil Walter)

The American glass industry in the course of its growth was subject to all the ailments that normally afflict infant industries. In addition, it had a number of its own special problems. In the first 130 years of the Colonies, only a half dozen attempts to establish glass factories were made, and they all seem to have ended disastrously. Given the temper of the times, this is not at all surprising.

In the first place, we must remember that the making of glass—unlike pottery, iron smelting, or woodworking—is an extremely complex and expensive procedure. It requires highly skilled artisans and specifically refined raw materials. For many years during the early life of this country, there were no locally trained glassmakers; consequently, workmen had to be brought over from Europe, and at wages far exceeding those paid most native employees—and naturally, the funds for such a luxury were not often available. Moreover, the policy of the British government—which controlled the economic life of the American Colonies—was specifically formulated to discourage colonial industry. The Crown was interested in selling English manufactured goods to the new settlers and obtaining for itself their abundant raw materials; it did not welcome the establishment in the Colonies of competing industries such as glassmaking. High taxes and severe export restrictions added to the troubles of those entrepreneurs unwise enough to challenge this policy. And

the challenges were few in the field of glass-making, since glass was for many years considered a luxury, not a necessity. Pewter, wood, and earthenware largely supplied the needs of the table and the pantry. Few besides the rich, in either Europe or America, could afford any glass beyond windowpanes and bottles.

Despite these odds, several attempts to set up glassmaking factories were made. Contemporary references indicate that glass was blown at the Jamestown, Virginia, settlement. Eight Dutch and Polish glassblowers arrived there in 1608, and a shop was established a mile or so from the young community. However, the original workers apparently died or left the colony, for in 1621 another six artisans, this time Italian, were sent to Jamestown. A manuscript dating from 1623 mentions glass sent home to England, so there appears to have been some production in that year. While there has been much speculation as to what this consisted of—with some authorities suggesting bottles and window glass and others opting for the colorful trade beads found in Indian graves of the period—no one really knows. And, of course, no items exist that can be traced to this first shop.

The Jamestown works ceased operation around 1625, and there appear to have been no further attempts in the Colonies until 1639, when a small plant was established at Salem, Massachusetts. This plant probably was never very successful, as a petition filed by its owners six years later indicates that they had not blown any glass for three years. In any case, the output doubtless was small, and none of it has been identified.

In New Amsterdam, now New York City, the craft seems to have met with more fortune. The Dutch encouraged colonial industries, and during the period 1650–1674

at least two glass factories operated at the tip of Manhattan Island. Colonial records contain frequent references to the men associated with these efforts—Johnnes Smedes, Evert Duycking, and the glassblowers Jansen and Dirkson—but no description of the factories or their products exists.

The same is true of Philadelphia's first glass factory. Joshua Tittery, an English window-glass maker, arrived in Philadelphia in 1683, and in the same year William Penn referred to a local glasshouse in a letter to its colonial proprietors. The shop appears to have been located about a mile and a half beyond what was then the city limits, in an area known as Shackamaxson. It was still in existence in 1691, but nothing made there has been identified.

It was not until after 1700 that the first truly successful American glass factory was organized. In 1717 Caspar Wistar arrived in this country as an immigrant from Germany. He settled in Philadelphia, where he became a prominent button manufacturer. Then, in 1739, he built a glass shop and began production on some two thousand acres of land that he owned in Salem County, New Jersey. Unlike most earlier proprietors, Wistar wisely provided for both fuel and transportation (through a series of creeks bisecting the land) as well as skilled foreign workers, four of whom were hired prior to the construction of the plant. In an agreement with these men, dated December 7, 1738, Wistar bound himself to

pay to Captain James Marshall fifty pounds and eight shillings sterling, the price of these men's passage from Rotterdam; they, to teach the art of glassblowing to him and his son Richard, and to no one else; and he, to provide land, fuel,

14

servants, food, and materials for a glass factory in the province of New Jersey, to advance money for all expenses including their support, and to give them one-third of the net profits of the enterprise.

That Wistar would agree not only to give these workmen a third of the net profits but also to fully support them gives some inkling of the difficulty colonial businessmen had in obtaining and keeping labor of this sort. That even under these terms the factory operated profitably until the Revolutionary War likewise indicates the kind of demand for glass that had developed by then. Caspar Wistar died in 1752, and his son succeeded to the business, running it until 1780.

As may be seen from the following notice, which was placed in the *Pennsylvania Chronicle and Universal Advertiser* for July 31, 1769, the factory produced a wide range of glassware:

Made at the Subscriber's Glass Works, now on hand and to be sold at his house in Market Street opposite the Meal Market, either wholesale or retail, between three and four hundred boxes of window glass consisting of the common sizes, viz. 10 by 12, 9 by 11, 8 by 10, 7 by 9, 6 by 8, &c. Lamp glasses or any uncommon sizes under 16 by 18 are cut on a short notice; where also may be had most sorts of bottles, gallon, half gallon and quart, full measure, half gallon cafe bottles, snuff and mustard bottles, receivers and retorts of various sizes, also electricity globes and tubes, &c.

As the above-mentioned glass is of American manufacture it is consequently

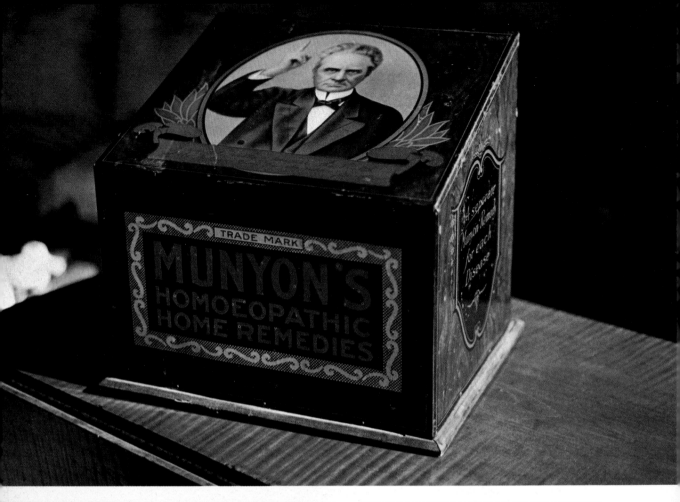

Top: Lithographed tin display case used in sale of proprietary medicines. *Above:* Lithographed tin tray with ad for Providence Brewing Company. (Both, courtesy Burton Spiller) *Right:* Green Swaim's Panacea, a common nineteenth-century proprietary. (Courtesy H. and B. Shatoff)

clear of the duties Americans justly complain of; and at present it seems particularly the interest of America to encourage her own manufacturers, especially those upon which duties have been imposed for the sole purpose of raising revenue. . . .

RICHARD WISTAR

The reference to the burden of duties placed on imported glass clearly reflects the onerous conditions under which American business labored in the years before the Revolution. Pleas similar to this were made by all glassmakers as well as by craftsmen in other fields. Not surprisingly, the public response was most fervent in times of high duties or short supply. At other times buyers showed a marked preference for imported glass, a condition that persisted well into the nineteenth century.

It is believed that most of the Wistar glass was a simple green or amber peasant ware of the kind then manufactured in Holland and Germany. No pieces are presently known that can without question be associated with the works, though attributions are made on the basis of history or fragments excavated at the site.

Wistar's glass sales in Philadelphia must have been in direct competition with another factory begun in that community around 1770. A notice appearing with his in the *Pennsylvania Chronicle* on July 31, 1769, advised the public that two pence per pound was being paid for broken flint glass, which "was intended to be worked up here at a new glass house." The anonymous proprietors also expressed the hope that "all lovers of American manufacture will encourage what lies in their power, and particularly in this instance, save, collect, and send such broken glass as above directed. . . . N.B. NO DUTIES HERE." It is possible that the

plant mentioned was the one built in the city's Kensington district in 1771 by Robert Towars and Joseph Leacock. Advertisements in various editions of the *Pennsylvania Journal* for 1773 indicate that the Philadelphia Glass Works, as it was known, was making green and white glassware as well as windowpanes. An extensive inventory was maintained that included decanters, all sorts of glasses, bottles, candlesticks, canisters, bird cisterns, lamp and candle shades, cruets, cream pots, dishes, ink cups, mustard pots, salts, and sugars.

The Philadelphia Glass Works was sold at auction in May 1780 to Thomas Leiper, a wine merchant who probably used the shop to make bottles for his wine. In any case, he ran it until 1800 when it was again sold. In 1824, Thomas W. Dyott, a famous maker of flasks and medicine bottles, acquired the controlling interest and occupied the premises until he went bankrupt in 1838. The factory continued in other hands until at least 1900 and possibly as late as 1926, making it one of the nation's longest-lived native industries.

New York City also had several glasshouses in the eighteenth century. A 1732 census report listed two, but nothing is known of them. Then, in 1751, four partners —Matthew Earnest, Samuel Bayard, Lodewyck Bemper, and Christian Hertell—contracted with a German glassblower, Johan Greiner, for the construction and operation of a glass factory, purchasing a tract of land for this purpose on the west side of Manhattan, in an area then known as New Found Land. The factory appears to have operated there for about ten years, and advertisements indicate a production of bottles from onequart to three-gallon capacity, including seal bottles, as well as chemical glass. The investors also owned a large tract of land at New Windsor, New York, and it seems that they had a second works there. However, no glass is known that may be attributed to either factory.

There was another glassworks in New Jersey, this one at a hamlet in Gloucester County that came to be called Glassboro. The new factory was established in 1780 by the three Stanger brothers, one of whom had been an apprentice to Richard Wistar of Philadelphia. The Stangers gave up the business within three years, after which the plant passed through numerous hands. In the second decade of the nineteenth century it became known as the Olive Glass Works, a reflection of its owners' predilection for green glass bottles. The plant prospered until 1824, when it was sold to the Harmony Glass Works, which had been established in 1813 a few hundred yards from the Olive Glass plant. The combined shops eventually became the Whitney Glass Company, which

was acquired in 1918 by the well-known Owens Bottle Company.

In terms of variety and quality of production, however, all these factories pale in significance beside the edifice erected by Henry William Stiegel, the premier American glassmaker of the period. Stiegel was born in Cologne, Germany, and migrated to Philadelphia in 1750. Two years later he fortuitously married the daughter of the owner of one of Pennsylvania's most profitable iron mines; and though his wife died in 1758 and he remarried within less than a year, Stiegel continued to operate her family's furnaces until 1763.

That year he built a small glasshouse at Elizabeth Furnace, Pennsylvania, seat of his iron-smelting wealth. Some bottles and window glass were made there, but it was really only a testing ground for bigger things to

Above: Glass candy container in the form of an early radio with traces of old paint. (Courtesy H. and B. Shatoff) *Opposite:* Variations of the basic long-neck bulbous body barber bottle, with hand-painted floral decoration. (Courtesy Emil Walter)

come. At Manheim, a nearby community that he built from the ground up, Stiegel established a works in 1765, and three years later he began construction of a larger factory at the same site. The first Manheim plant appears to have made little more than bottles and window glass, with simple tableware such as cream jugs and sugars thrown in for good measure, but Stiegel could not be satisfied with that. Putting the bulk of his considerable wealth into the business, he set out to produce flint-glass tableware of a quality equal to that of the best European centers.

The achievement of such a goal required highly trained workmen and carefully refined materials, all of which involved large sums of money. It is doubtful that Stiegel would have risked all on such a venture had it not been his feeling that the heavy import duties imposed by the Townshend Act of 1767 would drive all American trade to him.

His advertisement of July 29, 1771, in the *New York Gazette and Weekly Mercury* seems to bear out this reasoning in its blunt appeal to patriotic and financial motives:

American flint glass is now made at the factory in Manheim, in Lancaster County [Philadelphia], equal in quality with any imported from Europe, where all merchants, storekeepers, and others, may be supplied on very reasonable terms; and the proprietor of these works well knows the patriotic spirit of the Americans, he flatters himself they will encourage the manufactories of their own country, and hopes to be favored with their orders of Flint Glass, and begs leave to assure them that whatever commands he may receive shall, with great punctility, be executed....
HENRY WILLIAM STIEGEL

Extensive fund raising, lotteries, and advertising were employed to bolster the always shaky position of the new works, and the owner personally supervised all operations from his large mansion within sight of the factory's chimneys.

The variety of ware made here was on a scale never before seen in America. Account books for the period 1769–1770 list no less than forty-three different forms, including flint-glass decanters, tumblers, mugs, bowls, glasses, salts, sugars, butters, vials, inks, and jars. Molding, enameling, cutting, and engraving were all used in decoration, and so successfully did the workmen imitate current European style and quality that in most cases it is impossible to distinguish this glass from that blown at Bristol or the leading Continental factories.

This majestic venture lasted but five years. Mounting financial woes drove Stiegel to the wall, and in May of 1774 the plant

shut down. The owner was imprisoned for debt later that year; and though finally released, he lived out his life in obscurity. He died in 1785 in his former mansion, owned by a nephew who was once his employee.

The year of Stiegel's death another ambitious German glassmaker appeared on the American scene. John Frederick Amelung of Bremen chose Fredericktown, Maryland, for the site of his factory. He began construction there in 1785, completing a two-furnace house in 1787 and a second plant not far away before 1790. His initial capital was provided by a group of German investors, with later additions of native funds to a total of some £23,000, an immense sum in those days. As in Stiegel's case, the works was erected on a lavish scale. Over 2,000 acres of timberland were purchased to provide an ample fuel supply, and houses were built for an anticipated work force of 135 people. But, again, all proved to be in vain. Though it was without doubt the leading American glasshouse of its time, the factory failed in 1795, barely a decade after it began.

The New Bremen works, as it was known, was second only to Manheim in the quantity and variety of wares produced. A notice in the *Maryland Journal and Baltimore Advertiser* for May 16, 1789, noted that the proprietor "makes Window Glass, Transparent and Substantial, equal to London Crown, an inferior quality equal to Bristol Crown, all kinds of Flint Glass, such as Decanters and Wine Glasses; Tumblers of all sizes, and every other sort of Table Glass. He also cuts devices, Cyphers, Coats of Arms, or any other Fancy Figures in Glass." Surprisingly enough, in light of the history of contemporary factories, a good deal of this glass can now be positively identified. These include some marked pieces, such as a blown and engraved Pokal or covered goblet bearing the

incised inscription "New Breman Glass Manufactory–1788–North America, State of Maryland"; a covered flip glass inscribed "New Breman Glass Manufactory the 20th of June, 1788"; and another marked "Made at the Glass Manufactory of New Breman in Maryland the 23 Jan. 1789 by John Fr. Amelung & Company." Other pieces may be associated with these by style or family history, making for a very large body of recognized ware attributable to the Fredericktown plant.

Following the collapse of Amelung's plans, a group of his former employees entered into partnership with a wealthy young Swiss-American, Albert Gallatin, and his brother-in-law James Nicholson for the construction of a factory at New Geneva, Pennsylvania. This works, which was opened in 1797, was the first such venture west of the Allegheny Mountains. Though Gallatin and Nicholson sold out six years later, the plant and a successor works in the vicinity continued until destroyed by fire in 1847. Its principal output was window glass and green bottles, but both free- and mold-blown glasses, tumblers, bowls, sugars, and goblets were also manufactured. A surprisingly large number of these pieces have been handed down in families descended from the original workmen. Understandably, much of the authenticated ware is similar in hue and, particularly, in form to that made at the Amelung plant.

In contrast to all this activity in the mid-Atlantic colonies, New England had no glass factory at all in the hundred years following the failure at Salem. In 1752, however, Thomas Flucker and Isaac Winslow of Braintree, Massachusetts, established a small shop in their home community. Contemporary newspapers indicate that the workers were again imported from Germany and Holland,

and the plant carried on for seventeen years, despite several fires, until it was destroyed in a final disastrous conflagration in 1769.

Excavations have revealed that green and black glass spirits bottles were made at Braintree; and an advertisement in the *Boston Gazette and County Journal* for July 28, 1760, lists "snuff bottles, Pint, Quart, two Quart, and Gallon Bottles &c, also Pots for Pickles, Conserves of all sizes, likewise most sorts of Chymical Vessels" as among the items produced.

In East Hartford, Connecticut, there still stand the ruins of New England's best-known early glasshouse, the Pitkin works, established in 1783. In January of that year William and Elisha Pitkin and Samuel Bishop petitioned the General Assembly at Hartford for exclusive rights to carry on the glassworking trade in the state of Connecticut. Upon being granted a twenty-five-year monopoly, the proprietors set to work, finally erecting a factory in 1788. The business had its ups and downs, including early loss of its monopoly when it failed to make a sufficient amount of glass, but it continued through 1830. Included among its products were window glass, the earliest identified American figured flasks, and the flat, ovoid, finely ribbed flasks and bottles which, though produced elsewhere, came to be known by the generic name Pitkin Flasks.

There were just three other serious attempts at glassmaking during the eighteenth century. Sometime between 1785 and 1787 the first glass shop in upstate New York was erected at Dowesborough, a small community west of Albany. The venture was beset with difficulties and collapsed in 1789. Contemporary accounts indicate that window glass, demijohns, and pocket and snuff bottles were made there, but no examples have been found. The property was taken over by a second group of investors in 1792; they persevered until 1815, when the factory had to close because of a lack of fuel.

Meanwhile, a plant had been started in Boston in 1788. The owners encountered difficulty in constructing a proper building, and it was not until 1793 that production actually got under way. They also met with great difficulty in obtaining skilled artisans (a common occurrence with early glasshouses); and when the first group of blowers finally arrived from Germany, so the story goes, the populace was so delighted that they escorted the men through the streets from the pier to the shop. The Boston Crown Glass Manufactory remained active until 1827 and became famous for its window glass; the proprietors are also known to have produced hollow ware, though none of it is presently identifiable.

Late in the century Pittsburgh acquired its first factory, this one built in 1797 under the guidance of Gen. James O'Hara and Maj. Isaac Craig. O'Hara and Craig employed an experienced glassworker, William Eichbaum, and founded a successful business that continued under various managements for nearly a hundred years. It appears to have made window glass and a wide range of bottles and hollow ware.

Despite the economic dislocations produced by the Revolution and the War of 1812, the first quarter of the nineteenth century saw a sharp increase in the number of American glass factories. Particularly in New England and the Middle West, the new shops opened—and often closed—at an amazing rate.

In 1808 Bakewell and Page of Pittsburgh opened its doors. Built by Benjamin Bakewell and Edward Ensell, an English glassblower, it was the nation's first cut-glass factory. The firm passed through several managements prior to 1882, making a large number of different cut and engraved tablewares, as well as molded glass in clear and colored flint and, after 1825, pressed glass.

Bakewell and Page was for many years one of America's leading businesses. As early as 1817 the British traveler Elias Pym Fordham described the firm's products as equalling anything he had seen in England; and starting with the first exhibition in 1824, the company regularly took awards at Philadelphia's Franklin Institute. Its wares closely followed in form and style contemporaneous English and Irish glass and competed successfully on foreign and domestic markets.

In 1818 the Pittsburgh monopoly on cut glass was broken with the establishment in East Cambridge, Massachusetts, of the New England Glass Company. This firm's guiding light was Deming Jarves, a prolific glasshouse founder who was eventually involved in the establishment of no less than five Massachusetts factories. Just two years after its founding, the firm could boast of eighty employees and an annual output valued at $65,000. By 1823 the number of workers had nearly doubled, and the company was exporting glass to the West Indies and to various parts of South America.

The prosperity of the New England Glass Company continued uninterrupted until the late 1850s. In 1855 alone it could boast of an annual output totaling $500,000. However, increased domestic competition and labor unrest began to take effect in the decades following the Civil War. In 1878 the works was leased to William L. Libbey and his son Edward, who took over completely in 1883. A final strike in 1888 proved too much, and the business expired in that year, leaving behind a legacy of fine glass seldom rivaled in the history of this country.

During its long existence, this company manufactured every kind of glass demanded by the American public, from finely blown and cut flint to windowpane. As early as 1818 the *Hampshire Gazette* was praising its "elegant cut glass which would have done honor to the best manufactories in Europe." Its wares were sold and acclaimed throughout the world and regularly received awards for quality at the Franklin Institute, the Massachusetts Charitable Mechanics Association exhibit, and the American Institute of New York City. It made all sorts of blown ware, including three-piece mold, with lighting devices, decanters, castor sets, pitchers, bowls, and general tableware among the more popular items. At least two dozen different patterns in blown three-mold were utilized. In 1826, Henry Whitney and Enoch Robinson of the firm were granted a patent for a pressing machine; and pressed glass, particularly cup plates, became and long remained a New England specialty.

The leading American firm in the field of pressed glass, however, was the well-known Boston and Sandwich Glass Company, which was built at Sandwich, Massachusetts, in 1825 by Deming Jarves, who had at the time just terminated his relationship with the New England Glass Company. While its products included an extensive line of cut and blown three-mold ware as well as bottles, this company's reputation today is largely based on its production of lacy pressed glass; so much so, in fact, that the generic term "Sandwich glass" is applied to such ware even though it was made at many other factories. From 1827 until 1850, under Jarves's guidance, the plant specialized in pressed glass, shipping its products throughout the States and even to Europe and South America. Extensive excavations at Sandwich have made it possible to identify many of the

Green proprietary medicine bottle, embossed "L.O.C. Wishart's Pine Tree Tar Cordial, Phila., Patent 1859." (Courtesy Burton Spiller)

patterns utilized there, so that it is fairly easy for collectors to attribute pieces to that shop.

Sadly enough, the Sandwich works came to an end in the same year as its best-known competitor, the New England Glass Company, and for the same reasons: economic depression and labor troubles. A final strike and lockout in 1888 led to a shutdown in February of that year. Though several attempts were made to revitalize the works, none of them proved successful.

Another active fine wares maker of the early nineteenth century was the Jersey Glass Company of Jersey City. It was founded in 1824 and appears to have remained in business until around the time of the Civil War. The first proprietor, George Dummer, was a glass cutter, and his family appears to have controlled the business throughout its existence. Though relatively little is known about the output of this firm, the fact that its glass took prizes at both the Franklin Institute and the American Institute in New York City indicates a high level of quality. An advertising handbill circulated by the company reveals that it manufactured cut-glass decanters, glasses, dishes, salts, lamps, and candle shades as well as "Plain & Moulded Glass of all descriptions" and a wide variety of druggists' wares. Readily identifiable specimens include clear and green pressed salts embossed upon the base with the legend "Jersey Glass Co Nr N. York."

Although the above discussion may create the impression that after 1800 all United States glasshouses suddenly started to manufacture quantities of fine tableware, such, of course, was not the case. The overwhelming majority of these plants continued to make utilitarian bottles and window glass.

Among the better known of such works are the various establishments at Keene, New Hampshire. In 1815 the Marlboro Street Glass Works was opened at Keene for the manufacture of Pitkin-type flasks, historical flasks, and hollow ware, including decanters, pitchers, and inkwells. This mold-formed glass was patterned in geometric designs that are extremely popular with today's collectors. The Marlboro firm was successful enough to survive until 1841, an unusually long time for an isolated rural factory.

Another long-lived New England factory was the Coventry Glass Factory Company, erected at Coventry, Connecticut, around 1813 and active until 1850. This shop is known to have made chestnut bottles, inkstands blown in geometric-patterned three-piece molds, and snuff, blacking, porter, pickle, cologne, and proprietary medicine bottles, as well as demijohns, historical flasks, and tumblers.

The Willington Glass Company (1814–1872), at West Willington, Connecticut, was another prolific manufacturer of green and black glass. Preserve jars, porters, cathedrals, pickle, wine, and gin bottles, and figural flasks were among its many products, in addition to a few rare offhand pieces including witch balls, goblets, and candy holders.

In New York State, the Ellenville Glass Works was erected at Ellenville in 1836. It flourished for at least forty years. The incorporators here were a group of investors formerly connected with the West Willington factory. The Ellenville plant made hollow ware, carboys, demijohns, and fruit jars. Its output was substantial, reaching a gross of $300,000 in 1865, with over two hundred persons employed.

Another major factory was established at Lancaster, New York, in 1849. While this plant made many bitters and proprietary medicine bottles as well as free-blown pitchers, it is best known for a wide variety of historical flasks in half-pint, pint, and quart sizes, including cornucopias, scrolls, and pic-

Below: Barber bottles, blown in a mold and decorated with hand-painted floral designs. (Courtesy Emil Walter)

torials. Many of these were marked "Lancaster Glass Works."

In New Jersey there were several glass factories at Millville, best known of which was the one erected in 1806 by James Lee. It operated continuously until 1844, when it was sold to the Whitall brothers, becoming Whitall, Tatum and Company in 1857. The business, which is still active today, was once the nation's foremost producer of apothecaries' bottles. Its fruit jars are also justly famous among collectors.

Another well-known South Jersey glasshouse was the Harmony Glass Works. Built in 1813, it was purchased by Thomas H. Whitney in 1835 and became known as the Whitney Glass Works, the largest and most successful of the plants in its area. Historical flasks, the renowned Booz bottle, and many other types, including bitters and proprietary medicines, were made here, as well as hollow ware—bowls, pitchers, mugs, and glasses.

Farther west, there were early nineteenth-century glass manufactories in the Virginias and Ohio, among other states. In Ohio, Zanesville was the major glassmaking center. The first company there was established in 1815 and was producing hollow ware and druggists' bottles within a year. The White Glass Works, as it was called, lasted until 1851, surviving several changes of management and frequent shutdowns. It is known to have produced pitchers, sugar bowls, and salts as well as several much-sought-after figural flasks.

A second Zanesville plant was built in 1816 by Peter Mills, James Hanson, and James and Peter Culbertson, who were all experienced glassmen from the Pittsburgh area. It became known as the New Granite Glass Company and continued under various owners through 1849. Tableware was made here to some extent, as there is at least one decanter in existence marked "Murdock & Casell,

Zanesville," a partnership of the 1830s. However, bottles, including historical flasks, were the major items offered to the public.

Other Ohio shops were located at Mantua and Kent in Portage County. The Mantua Glass Company opened in 1822 and appears to have made a rather substantial amount of blown three-mold ware as well as Pitkin-type and figural flasks. It lasted only seven years. One of its owners, David Ladd, also established the first factory at Kent, in 1824, which produced blown three-mold dishes and bottles.

The factories discussed here, while important, are only a small portion of the plants that existed in the United States during the last century. The business continued to expand throughout the 1800s and is now a major American industry, though, like most such enterprises, it has come to be concentrated in a relatively small number of large operations. The days of the independent glassmaker came to an end in the late 1800s; today, he is just a factory worker performing some small step in the automated manufacturing process. The bottles and hollow ware made by these craftsmen have survived, however, to remind us of the creative skill and determination of our forebears.

2
How a Bottle Is Made

Above: Artist's representation of late-nineteenth-century glass factory. (Courtesy N.Y. Public Library) *Opposite:* Typical glassmakers' tools. At left, shears; at right, a device for finishing bottle necks. (Courtesy Staten Island Historical Society)

Bottles were without doubt among the very first articles manufactured from glass. The origin of their production, however, like that of glass in general, is shrouded in mystery. Historians disagree as to whether Egypt or Syria should be credited with the first successful glass manufacture. The discovery of a glasshouse site in upper Egypt dating to 1400 B.C. leaves no doubt as to the antiquity of the craft in that country, and glass beads from the same era has been found in the Near East. We can at least say that the craft was well known throughout the ancient world.

The earliest glass vessels were made in molds, and it was not until the Syrians invented the blowpipe around 300 B.C. that the true possibilities of the craft began to be realized. The Romans, here as in so many other areas of the arts, were the first major creative force. After importing their early glass from Egypt and Syria, they began, in the first century A.D., to create a wide variety of glass forms and decorative techniques, including glass cutting and the use of numerous molds. Cameo, mosaic, filigree, and cased glass were all developed in Roman shops, and for hundreds of years Rome supplied the civilized world with its bottles and other glass.

With the decline of the Roman Empire all this came to an end. The Eastern Empire continued the craft; but in the West, the glasshouses vanished under the heels of the barbarian hordes. A few glassblowers fled to

26

the forests of Germany, and by the fifth century A.D. had founded the tiny shops that for the next thousand years constituted Europe's sole contribution to glassmaking history. Once again the real center of glassmaking shifted to the east, to Syria and particularly to Constantinople, where the Roman and Eastern traditions had blended in a highly developed industry.

It was probably from here that the first glassmakers were brought to Venice to establish the famous shops there. As great merchants and craftsmen in their own right, the Venetians were quick to recognize the trade potential in the glass industry. By the middle of the thirteenth century their manufactories were the most important in Europe, and when Constantinople fell before the Turks in 1453, Venetian wares stood unchallenged. A great many different techniques were employed in the island shops of Venice, including blowing and molding with gilded, enameled, or applied decoration. Among the glass types developed were agate, millefiori, and latticinio.

Like the Romans and Byzantines before them, the Venetians took great pains to protect the secrets of their trade monopoly, even to the extent of putting to death absconding glassblowers, but it was of no avail. As workers were lured into other countries, the craft spread across Europe. The English developed lead glass in the seventeenth century, the French and Dutch provided important contributions to the craft, and the German forest shops, after hundreds of years of making green glass bottles, began cutting, engraving, and enameling in the manner soon to be known worldwide as Bohemian.

Since artisans from all these areas came to America, it is understandable that early American glass displays characteristics that

Left: Early pattern-molded bottles. At left, amber New England Pitkin bottle; at right, aqua swirl bottle from Ohio. (Courtesy Jim Wetzel)
Top: Engraver decorating a goblet. *Above:* Glassmakers applying handle to a pitcher. (Both, courtesy N.Y. Public Library)

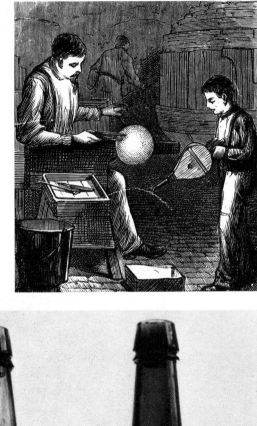

may be associated with several different countries. In all cases, however, the basic materials and techniques were similar.

All glass is made from a mixture of silica —usually in the form of sand—and an alkali, such as potash, lime, or carbonate of soda. When this combination—known in the trade as a "batch"—is subjected to intense heat, it melts, the alkali serving as a flux to produce a fusion of the other materials. The resultant mixture is a viscous near-liquid which may be molded or blown into many shapes.

The most basic type of glass and the one most often used for bottles is common green glass. It is neither artificially colored nor rendered colorless by the addition of manganese, and consequently may vary in hue from pale blue through various greens and ambers, depending on the various metallic impurities found in the raw materials. It is, moreover, the cheapest of all glass and consequently has been employed from the very first days of American glassmaking right up to today.

Better-quality bottles, such as druggists' and chemical wares, and hollow ware, such as decanters and bar bottles, were made from soda glass. In this compound, carbonate of lime replaced potash as the alkaline base, while manganese oxide was added to neutralize the hues produced by impurities in the batch. Soda glass was more expensive and took more skill to make, so that it was not widely used in bottle making until the 1880s, when consumers began to demand clear bottles.

Lead or flint glass is manufactured from a mixture of sand, potash, and oxide of lead, with the usual addition of the manganese decolorizer. It fuses at a lower temperature than the other forms of glass, is more plastic and hence easier for the worker to manipulate, and is more brilliant than soda glass. Its softness made this ware most suitable for

cutting and engraving. Thus, it was widely used in tableware, though generally not for bottles other than decanters.

All glass types can be artificially colored by the addition of various metallic oxides, and even the earliest American shops employed a certain amount of colored glass, chiefly for tablewares and decorative bottles such as pocket and historical flasks. In the first years, up to about 1830, the colors used were rather limited, consisting chiefly of blues (produced by the addition of cobalt), iron-based greens, and purples or amethysts (achieved by adding manganese, which in certain proportions acts as a colorizing rather than a decolorizing agent). An increase in the availability of artificial colorants led, in the last half of the nineteenth century, to a much wider range of hues, many of which may be seen in the art-glass barber bottles shown in this chapter, made both here and abroad.

Key to the production of any glass is the oven or furnace in which the batch is melted. The earliest ovens were rectangular structures with open fire pits. An annealing oven in similar form was employed for the slow cooling process necessary to keep new glass from shattering. It appears that such boxlike ovens were used for thousands of years—the one unearthed at Tel el Amarna in Egypt, which dates to the fourteenth century B.C., differs little from that shown in a fifteenth-century painting of a Flemish glasshouse. By the 1600s, however, most workers were using a round, two-chamber furnace, in which the lower level served as a fire box and the upper as a heating chamber in which pots of batch were placed for melting.

These pots or crucibles are of great importance in glassmaking. They are made from a mixture of finely powdered clay and grog, which is ground fragments of old pots, carefully worked to eliminate air pockets whose presence would cause a pot to shatter when heated, resulting in the loss of expensive materials. The pots are built up coil fashion, allowed to age, then fired to the desired hardness. Early pots were open and looked a bit like huge handleless tea cups. In the nineteenth century these were largely replaced by hooded pots, some of which were designed to hold as much as a ton and a half of melted glass, or "metal," as it is termed in the trade.

A third type of glassmaker's oven—the kind first employed in this country—was the so-called beehive, an oval structure consisting of three divisions or chambers; the lowest of these was the fire box, the center section held the pots, and the upper section was used for annealing. Arched windows of various sizes allowed access to the oven and its pots so that the workers could draw off glass as needed. In the course of time this form also was modified, primarily in regard to its flue system, largely because coal was introduced as a replacement for wood in heating the furnace.

The process by which a bottle is made is a long and frequently tedious one. First, the oven and the pots have to be heated to the proper point. Then the pots are filled with the batch, which is allowed to melt for thirty to forty hours until it is completely fluid. Throughout this period workmen have to stand by to remove impurities, which float to the surface of the pots as a white porous scum. If left, these impure salts could ruin the pots or cause bubbles in the glass; hence, considerable effort is devoted to disposing of them.

After the glass has vitrified and been allowed to cool a bit to a viscous and more workable state, the glassblower inserts his blowpipe through one of the apertures or windows in the oven and withdraws a glob of molten glass. As may be seen from the illustration, the pipe is a hollow iron tube wider at the gathering than at the blowing end. It is generally four to six feet long.

The glob or gather of glass is first rolled on a polished stone slab, called a marver, to give it an even surface so that on expansion the metal will be of uniform-thickness. The workman then takes the pipe in his mouth and, turning it continuously to preserve a symmetrical shape, expands it by blowing air into the bag of molten metal—much as a child blows up a piece of bubble gum. Since the gather cools quickly it is often necessary to put the pipe back in the furnace for a few moments while the gather is being shaped.

If the piece is being free-blown the artisan then inserts it in a pocket, shaped something like a quarter section of grapefruit, in a wooden block. The block is kept wet to avoid charring, and by turning the gather of glass (now called a parison) in the block, the worker assures that it will be symmetrical. Sitting in a specially constructed chair, the worker then shapes the body of the bottle by manipulation and with aid of a pincer-shaped tool called a pucellas. With it he might elongate the container's neck, constrict or otherwise alter its body shape, or even snip it off at a given point. The container bottom is flattened by rubbing it across a breadboard-shaped piece of wood called a battledore.

Finally, the bottle must be necked. To do this it is initially removed from the blowpipe, usually by applying a drop of water to the hot glass so that it will crack off. An assistant first brings another iron rod—called a pontil or punty rod—about the length of the blowpipe. One end of the pontil contains a small gather of hot glass. When this is pressed against the bottom of the bottle, the two adhere, providing a way in which the still-hot bottle can be held while the neck is separated from the blowpipe and finished. Shears and lipping devices are employed for this job.

Fire extinguisher bottle, milk glass with molded floral decoration. (Courtesy H. and B. Shatoff)

The earliest bottles tend to have very simple lips, cut straight off and fire-polished or smoothed by reinsertion in the oven. This, of course, was the fastest way, but it had drawbacks. Being unreinforced, such necks broke easily. Moreover, they were not particularly attractive, nor did they take corks well. Accordingly, most bottles from 1840 on were finished with one of several lippers.

The last step in making the bottle is to break off the pontil, again by using a drop of water. This leaves a rough circular scar on the bottle base, which is known as a pontil scar and is commonly seen on bottles made in this country before 1850.

Since pontil marks are unsightly and in some cases cause the container to sit unevenly, they were frequently filed off, particularly on decanters and cologne bottles where appearance was considered important. Shortly before 1850, some shops began to employ a bare iron pontil, that is, a rod not containing any hot glass. The rod had a flared tip and when heated red hot it would, if pressed against the base of the bottle, adhere to it. The use of this kind of pontil may be easily recognized by the circular impression and the fragments of oxidized iron left on the base of the bottle. Though such pontils were used for all sorts of bottles, they seem to be most common on sodas and minerals.

The period of the iron pontil was relatively brief, lasting for little more than twenty years and overlapping the development of the final and most effective gripping tool. This was the snap case, a double-branched iron rod with a metal cup set between the arms. The bottle bottom is placed in the cup, and a sliding ring draws the arms together, providing a gentle and secure holder while the neck is finished. Snap cases were introduced in American shops soon after 1850, and by 1870 their use was practically universal. Most bot-

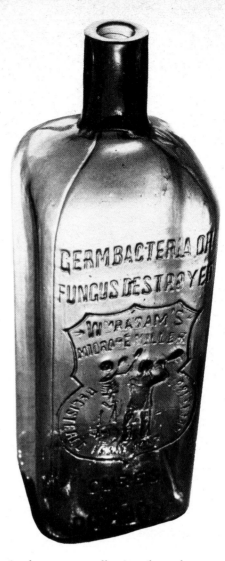

tles in the average collection show the smooth bottom associated with use of this device.

While free blowing of bottles had advantages in terms of the wide variety of forms that might be achieved, it also had distinct disadvantages. The method was slow, and as the need for bottles increased it became necessary to find ways to speed up production. Moreover, free-formed bottles were seldom uniform in capacity, a matter of great importance to merchants. Commercial interests also needed a bottle that could be personally identified with the name of a product or a producer. This, too, was not possible with free-blown containers.

Accordingly, American glass workers turned more and more to the use of molds.

Simple molds were known before the first century A.D., but it was not until the 1700s that efficient hinged brass and iron forms were developed. These were widely used in Europe but did not gain extensive acceptance in this country until after 1800. Prior to that time, our craftsmen employed several types of nonshoulder molds, that is, molds that formed only the body of the bottle.

The best known of these is the dip mold, a cuplike receptacle often set into the floor of the factory. To use the dip mold, the worker would remove a gather of glass from the oven and, placing it in the mold, would blow into the pipe to expand the metal. Since the top of the mold was larger than the base, the fully expanded bottle could readily be withdrawn.

It was then necessary to finish the shoulder, neck, and lip of the vessel in the traditional manner as previously discussed.

In one respect the hinged mold was an improvement over such previous techniques. By cutting perpendicular grooves into the interior sides of the mold, it became possible to blow a pattern into the bottle. Many Stiegel-type flasks were decorated in this manner. The standard method of pattern molding was known as the half-post technique and involved two steps. The gather of glass was expanded once in the form, then removed and redipped in a second coating of hot glass, after which it was again blown in the mold. A variety of patterns could be produced by employing molds of different

Free-blown New England chestnut bottles in
various shades of green. Bottle in foreground
is only known example from Temple, N.H., glass
factory, ca. 1780. (Courtesy Robert Anderson)

patterns for the two dippings or by twisting the bottle upon the second removal to produce a swirled overlay.

The first hinged molds introduced in this country were of the nonshoulder type, simple metal cylinders hinged at one side. Since they did not extend the full length of the bottle, it was still necessary for the artisan to hand-finish the upper portions. But they did answer a major need of the commercial bottle user, the demand for embossed bottles. By cutting lettering into the interior of the mold, a bottle could be blown bearing the identification of its source or contents, thus eliminating the need for paper labels. Since the parts of the mold did not fit together completely, receptacles produced in them show a mold seam along each side, where the glass was forced out the crack in the process of expansion. Such seams also appear in later mold-formed bottles and provide useful information about the type of mold involved and, to some extent, about the age of the vessel.

The mass production demanded by conditions of nineteenth-century industrialism did not allow, however, for the time required to finish containers blown in nonshoulder molds. The development of full-size forms was therefore a natural step. These molds were hinged and, generally, in two or three sections. In either case, they produced bottles that were completely shaped, except at the bottle mouth. It was there that the blowpipe was attached, so that it was still necessary to break that off and then finish the lip. Full-size molds were, like the earlier type, cut to provide commercial embossments; many had an opening in one side into which plates bearing the names of various merchants or products could be inserted. By use of these plate molds the same form could be utilized for many different bottles, at a great saving to the manufacturer and thus to the consumer. The development

of the plate mold coincided with the patent medicine boom of the 1870s, and it reflected the interest in advertising that enveloped commercial interests during that period.

Improved methods of cutting molds also resulted in use of molds that varied in shape and in internal decoration, so that a wide variety of bottles replaced the standard cylinders previously in circulation.

Interestingly enough, though, certain bottle users wanted an entirely plain bottle. Wine bottlers in the last twenty years of the nineteenth century insisted on vessels that were rotated in the mold prior to removal in order to erase the mold seams. In order to facilitate this, the mold was dipped in water and its interior coated with a slick paste. "Turn-mold" bottles may be recognized by their lack of seams and by tiny concentric scratch lines about the body where the turning bottle scraped against the interior of the mold. They often are highly polished; but as they lack any sort of embossment, they are not in great favor with most collectors.

With the development of the Owens automatic bottle-making machine in 1903, the glassblower's role came to an end as far as commercial containers were concerned. While collectors are beginning to show some interest in machine-made bottles, particularly in areas where older forms are scarce, most hobbyists continue to prefer those vessels that show somewhere, if only in the lip or mouth of the bottle, the hand of the craftsman.

Of course, in the area of pressed glass, the machine had intruded long before 1900. In the last quarter of the eighteenth century, British and Dutch glasshouses had begun to employ simple hand presses to form the feet for condiment bottles and other vessels. A glob of hot glass was gathered on the pontil rod and held over the open mold. The proper quantity was then cut off and allowed to fall into the mold, which was then pressed together manually like a large pair of pliers.

Presses of this sort were introduced into the United States around 1800 and were used extensively in the making of decanter stoppers. Then, around 1825, mechanical presses began to appear. There is some dispute as to which American glasshouse should be credited with first putting these devices into production, but there is no doubt that the invention is of United States origin. The first patent, for the making of pressed-glass furniture knobs, was taken out by John P. Bakewell of Pittsburgh's Bakewell and Page in 1825. A year later Henry Whitney and Enoch Robinson of the New England Glass Company at Cambridge, Massachusetts, obtained a monopoly for manufacture of a similar machine.

These early presses were limited to the making of simple, shallow forms such as cup plates and bowls. Accordingly, their products are of only academic interest to the bottle collector. In November of 1830, however, John M'Gann of the Kensington Glass Works obtained a patent for a mechanical press sufficiently sophisticated to make "all kinds of bottles, Decanters and other pressed hollow Glassware, with the neck or aperture smaller than the cavity or inside diameter of the vessel." The device was intended to function as follows:

When a decanter or similar vessel is to be made, there are to be two moulds, with their proper presses. In one mould the lower part of the decanter is formed, in the other the upper part and neck. One of the moulds is fixed to a hinge in such a way, that when the cores (plungers) of the two parts are withdrawn, one mould will turn over upon the other and bring the edges of the glass into exact contact, when by a slight pressure they are made to adhere; the moulds are then opened and the decanter removed from it.

Needless to say, the development of such a machine had a profound effect on the American glass industry. Glass tablewares had never been cheap, and most households, particularly prior to 1820, had only a few bottles, glasses, and the like. As the pressing machine spread throughout the industry during the 1830s and 1840s, manufacturers began to offer a wide variety of inexpensive pressed objects.

Deming Jarves's Boston and Sandwich Glass Company was one of the leaders in the field and the company with whom pressed glass is most often associated. It produced great quantities of lovely, multihued perfume, cologne, toilet, pomade, and ointment jars. Many of the perfume bottles were made in the same presses used to make lamp fonts and bowl bases. The pomade and ointment jars were created in highly sophisticated figural forms, including that of a small bear sitting on its haunches.

While pressed glass is not of major importance to most collectors, since there are only a limited number of bottles made in that medium, we should remember that in addition to Sandwich, many glass factories made such pieces (particularly decanters), including Bakewell and Page and the well-known New England Glass Company.

It need hardly be said that the mechanically pressed and blown glass of the late nineteenth and early twentieth centuries was a far cry from the simple offhand pieces formed by our country's early artisans. It is always with a bit of regret that the ardent bottle lover handles an early pontiled bottle, knowing that it is an artifact of a craft that is, for the most part, long dead in this country.

3
WINE & SPIRITS BOTTLES

Above: Handled whiskey jugs. From left to right: Chestnut Grove Whiskey; A. M. Binninger & Co.; W. B. Crowell Star Whiskey. *Opposite:* Blue frosted glass whiskey bottle in form of a turn-of-the-century golfer. (All, courtesy Burton Spiller)

A wide variety of bottles was used to contain wine and various types of alcoholic beverages. Most collectors concentrate on one category in this field, rather than trying to gather together all forms.

The first type of spirits to be discovered was wine. Grapes were cultivated for fermentation in the Near East as long ago as 2000 B.C., and archeological excavations in that area have disclosed numerous glass and ceramic containers clearly intended for storing and transporting wine. The techniques of viniculture were later carried into France and Germany by the Roman armies; and from the Middle Ages on, most Continental countries produced wine, sherry, and brandy.

More potent alcoholic drinks were developed at a later date. Gin was not discovered until the seventeenth century, while bourbon appeared a century later. Accordingly, the earliest bottles with which we are concerned are ones that served primarily as receptacles for wine or its fortified derivatives. During the period that American collectors are primarily interested in—1650–1850—there was a gradual but clearly detectable change in form.

The earliest wine and spirits bottles in America were free-blown, bulbous, long-necked vessels with a shallow indentation or kickup and pronounced pontil scar. Examples of these have been found in Indian graves, but since there were no glasshouses in operation here during the period they were popular, it

is extremely doubtful that any could have been made in America. About 1660, a short, squat bottle with much less neck and a deep kickup appeared; and a hundred years later the neck had grown longer, the kickup even deeper, and the vessel as a whole much taller. Finally, by 1860, the straight-sided cylindrical molded container, which is the prototype of modern wine and whiskey bottles, emerged. It need hardly be said that there were many variations from the general line of development, and some of these will be discussed in detail. It is, however, helpful to have some idea of the basic trend.

These vessels are specimens of the so-called English tradition in manufacture of wine and spirits, as opposed to the Dutch or Continental form. Two groups of the latter are shown (page 45); they may generally be distinguished from the English bottles by the following characteristics: longer necks, much higher basal kickups, and larger pontil scars. Early vessels from the British Isles also have a narrow, disklike collar as opposed to the flat, wraparound finish on the Continental examples. One Continental example is of particular interest. It is a very squat, egg-shaped container with flat sides. Written in ink on its protective leather cover is the legend "Nova Espana, 1682, Olid," an indication that the bottle may have belonged to one of the Conquistadors.

Since so many early wine and spirits containers were imported from Europe and since all of them tend to be very similar, it is hard to determine which, if any, were made in this country. Excavations at the site of the Germantown Glass Works, active near Braintree, Massachusetts, from 1752 until 1768, have uncovered fragments of such vessels in the 1750 form. These show the typical English kickup and disklike or wafer collar. An advertise-

ment for the Germantown works published in the April 4, 1761, edition of the *Boston News-Letter* noted that it produced "pint, quart, two quart and gallon bottles"; it may be assumed that these were similar in form to the excavated examples. Also, a bottle has been found that bears a seal stamped "Wm. Savery, 1762." Savery was a famous eighteenth-century Philadelphia cabinetmaker; and while it is possible that he had this vessel blown in England, it is more likely that it was made in Caspar Wistar's Salem County, New Jersey, glass factory. A 1752 inventory of Wistar's shops lists "round bottles" in half-gallon, gallon, and quart sizes.

While not numerous, bottles affixed with seals—that is, globs of hot glass impressed with dates and the initials or full names of owners—can often be of great importance in determining origins. The practice of sealing bottles originated in England during the 1600s. At first individuals, then taverns, shippers, merchants, and distillers had their containers customized in this manner. While most seal bottles may be traced to the British Isles or to Europe, the form was also common in North America. An advertisement for the New Windsor, New York, glasshouse appearing in the *New York Gazette* for October 19, 1754, offered accommodation to "all gentlemen that wants bottles of any size with their names on them." A fragment of a seal bottle dug up at the Germantown site carries the stamp "IQ," believed to be the cipher of Jonathan Quincy, who was related to one of the early partners in the glass factory. At a later date, bottles with seals impressed "JL" and "MM/Mt Vernon Glass Co." were made at the old bottle factory active at Mount Vernon, New York, from 1810 to 1844. These, of course, are rather late representations of the classic type.

Milk glass cordial or whiskey bottle in form of the base of the Statue of Liberty, surmounted by bronze figurine. (Courtesy Burton Spiller)

CHESTNUT BOTTLES

From 1750 to 1850 American wine and spirits containers gradually grew taller and more cylindrical, but one archaic form remained. This was the chestnut bottle. These ubiquitous vessels were made in all sizes—from two-inch miniatures to mammoth twenty-gallon carboys—and in all shades of aqua, green, and amber. In the smaller dimensions, they are the simplest type of vessel to make, being essentially the form that naturally results when a gather of glass is expanded and then swung on the end of a blowpipe. As may be seen in the illustrations, the result is a bulbous, long-necked shape. Most chestnuts were finished by pushing the base in a bit to form a kickup and then laying a thin band of glass around the rim to strengthen the collar.

The term "chestnut" refers to the fact that if the form is slightly flattened, as it often was, it bears a resemblance to the American chestnut. Such bottles were also called Ludlow bottles, reflecting a traditional belief that they were once manufactured at the Ludlow Glass Factory near Springfield, Massachusetts. It has not been determined that such vessels were in fact made at Ludlow, but the form was probably a staple of all the early shops. Fragments have been found at the Coventry and Glastonbury, Connecticut, factories as well as at Keene, New Hampshire, and Mount Vernon, New York. The example in the foreground of the photograph on page 36 is the only known specimen to have a history of having been blown at the Temple, New Hampshire, glasshouse, which operated only two years, from 1780 to 1782.

Despite their relative abundance, chestnuts are not recognizable in early inventories and advertisements, because normally they were referred to only by capacity; the terms

Opposite: European-style wine and spirits bottles dating from the seventeenth and eighteenth centuries. Leather-covered bottle is dated 1682 and is from Spanish Florida. (Courtesy Robert Anderson)

"chestnut" and "Ludlow" were coined by collectors at a much later date.

DEMIJOHNS AND CARBOYS

The largest vessels in the chestnut form are, however, frequently mentioned in early documents, and are often treated as a separate class. These are demijohns and carboys.

One of the earliest references to demijohns occurs in the *Columbian Centinel* of Boston for December 17, 1788. The Pitkin Glass Works of East Hartford, Connecticut, placed the following ad for its products in this category:

GLASS MANUFACTORY

Mr. Hewes . . . takes this method to inform his friends and the publick that they may be supplied with . . . DIME-JOHNS or any other large bottles by leaving their names and the size and form of said bottles with Mr. William Cunningham near Liberty Pole.

Demijohns, it should be noted, are quite different in form from carboys, though both served approximately the same purpose. The former are bulbous with rather long necks, while the latter, further removed from the chestnut shape, are cylindrical with short necks. Demijohns are probably the older type, though both have been made for hundreds of years. The earliest examples are free-blown with high kickups and large open pontils. Since it was extremely difficult to blow vessels as large as these, molds, particularly for carboys, were developed in the late 1700s. One such mold was listed among the assets of the Westford Glass Company of Westford, Connecticut, at the time of its failure in 1865.

Demijohns, also, were usually covered with a wicker sheath to avoid breakage. Another interesting entry in the Westford inven-

Top right: Miniature New England chestnut bottles in shades of green, none over 6″ high. (Courtesy J. and L. Kindler) *Right:* Whiskey bottles in shades of amber. From left to right: Monk's Old Bourbon Whiskey; Constitutional Beverage; E. G. Booz's Old Cabin Whiskey. (Courtesy Burton Spiller)

tory was a reference to "about 215 half gallon demi-johns at Mrs. Geo. Chapman's to cover," an obvious indication that the weaving of the rattan jackets was often farmed out to nearby families rather than done in the factory. A price list of the New England Glass Bottle Company of East Cambridge, Massachusetts, dated November 1, 1829, lists wickered demijohns in ten sizes, from one to ten gallons. The smallest of these vessels cost forty cents apiece, the largest $1.30. These were substantial sums, so it is understandable that the containers were reused as long as they remained intact. Carboys were probably not given a wicker sheath in most cases. There are no references to such sheaths in the early notices; and it is known that some carboys, at least, were shipped in specially designed wooden boxes. The New England Glass price list, previously mentioned, boasted of no less than twenty sizes in carboys, from one gallon to giants twenty times that size. Carboy prices were substantially lower than those asked for demijohns—a quarter for the gallon and a dollar for the ten-gallon size—a difference that may well reflect the added expense of wickering the latter.

While they were no doubt used to store and transport various liquids, such as cooking oil, vinegar, and molasses, demijohns and carboys figured most prominently in the liquor trade. Thus, the Hartford merchant Frederick Bull could call the public's attention to the fact that he had on hand "A FEW DEMIJOHNS of very fine old Holland Gin, India Brandy, Jamaica and Antigua Spirit and India Madiera Wine . . . Selected expressly for the sick. For sale at the sign of The Good Samaritan" (*Connecticut Courant,* March 31, 1829).

Early demijohns and carboys are found in dark green to black glass with an occasional one in amber. In the nineteenth cen-

tury, particularly after 1850, pale green, aqua,
and clear glass became more common. Examples from the later period are quite common; the collector interest centers on the
larger bottles, whose huge size makes them
suitable for interior decorating.

HANDLED WHISKEY JUGS

Another interesting relative of the chestnut bottle is the handled whiskey bottle or
jug. Some of these are of a distinctly chestnut shape. These are not necessarily the oldest examples, though. The round-ribbed jug
with a seal impressed "JFT & Co/Philadel-
phia" that has been found has an eighteenth-
century history, and similar specimens were
pattern-molded at the Stiegel glass factory
around 1765–1774.

These jugs were extremely popular during the nineteenth century as containers for
bourbon whiskey, which was first made in
Bourbon County, Kentucky, in the late eighteenth or early nineteenth century. Bourbon
is composed of at least 51 percent corn mash
plus malt and rye and has been a popular
American stimulant for many years. The
earliest containers are free-blown with open
pontils and applied handles, while later pieces
are mold-formed, as is the case with the fine
ribbed jug with a spout shown on p. 36. It
bears a seal stamped "Star Whiskey New
York/WB Crowell." Crowell was a major
New York City liquor distributor, and several
unusual bottles bearing his name are known.

A large number of handled whiskeys bear
an embossed manufacturer's or dealer's mark
or, in some cases, a seal similarly impressed.
In fact, after 1825, it is upon these bottles
that seals most commonly appear.

Unlike chestnuts, demijohns, and carboys, which were almost always plain and
unmarked by embossments, decorative or
otherwise, handled jugs are often embossed

and are collected for this as well as for their
form and color. Most specimens are a shade
of amber, but other hues such as yellow, red,
green, and puce do appear.

Though even today most bourbon is
made in Kentucky and a few other southern
states, distribution and advertising has been
nationwide since before the Civil War. The
manufacturers felt they had a good thing and,
like most contemporary merchants, didn't
hesitate to say so, even if it meant buying
space in a newspaper clear across the country.
The following notice in a California paper is
representative:

J. B. CABLE O.P.S.
MONOGRAM WHISKEY
It is strictly hand-made sour mash on the
purity of which you can depend. It is by
no means a cheap whiskey and in buying
you have to consider that you buy and
pay for a first-class article. Hon. J. B.
Cable, Nelson Co., Kentucky, guarantees
every drop of liquor sold by him or
through his agents as strictly pure, old and
mellow.

(*The Morning Press*, Santa Barbara,
April 14, 1893)

Very little has changed with bourbon since
1893. Cable's sucessors still advertise extensively, and their whiskey remains the American liquor.

WINES

The tall, cylindrical wine bottles of the
nineteenth century are by and large less interesting than their predecessors. The need
for large numbers of these containers led to
the introduction of dip and full-size molds
and a consequent similarity among pieces. At
the time of the Westford Glass Company's
failure in 1865, there were four such molds

among the effects of the corporation—a No. 5, two No. 6s, and a No. 7. In each case the number indicated what portion of a gallon could be contained in the bottle to be produced; for example the No. 5 mold made a fifth.

These bottles were turned out in great numbers at factories throughout the country. The New England Glass Bottle Company listed several varieties in an 1829 price list, including quarts at $8.50 per gross and pints in the same quantity for $7.50. One-quart claret bottles were available at $9.00 a gross and champagnes in the same size for $10.00. Nearly four decades later, in 1866, the Willington Glass Company of West Willington, Connecticut, sold No. 5, 5½, and 6 wines at prices ranging from $8.00 to $12.50 per gross, indicating that the price structure in the industry had not changed greatly in the interim. Most of the later receptacles were no doubt unembossed "turn-mold" bottles, so called from the fact that they were rotated in the mold to remove the mold seam marks and to give the piece a shiny patina. This technique was possible because unlike liquor merchants, whose bottles were highly embossed, wine merchants chose to use paper labels.

Some of the late nineteenth-century bottles were of substantial size. One example is known that is fully seventeen inches high. One may appreciate its massive dimensions by comparing it to a standard, full-size fifth.

Color in turn-mold wines can be most spectacular. Teal, red, blue, and various shades of aqua are seen. Amber and green are, however, most common.

American wine growers have always had to cope with a general prejudice in favor of European wines, and this was particularly true in the early days of the industry. Thus, in 1868, the Pleasant Valley Wine Company

Eighteenth-century demijohns in shades of green. Example at far left is from New England; the others are European. (Courtesy Robert Anderson)

of Hammondsport, New York, found it necessary to point out that its "Celebrated American Wines are . . . equal to those imported and are sold at much lower prices" (*Connecticut Courant,* March 31, 1868). A year later European vineyards were ravaged by an American insect infestation and would have been completely destroyed, had it not been possible to import resistant American roots onto which the European grape varieties could then be grafted.

CASE BOTTLES

One form of tall spirits bottle has traditionally been associated with the bottling of rum and gin. This is the case bottle, a square container tapering in toward the base with high shoulder and short neck. The term "case" refers to the fact that these vessels, which were originally used by chemists or apothecaries, were often packed in a wooden case of four to twelve for safe keeping in transit. An exceedingly rare example of an actual case is the painted pine chest with its four original bottles. This set was found in New England completely intact and dates from around 1835.

For many years it was thought that most if not all case bottles found in this country were imported. While it is true that large numbers were shipped here full of Dutch gin or Jamaica rum, recent research has shown that the form was a common product of American glasshouses. Caspar Wistar's inventory of 1752 lists twenty-five dozen half-gallon case bottles (valued at £11, 5s.), and it is known that they were also made between 1752 and 1768 at the Germantown Glass Works in Braintree, Massachusetts. Such containers were also advertised in 1777 by the Philadelphia Glass Works.

Many of the foreign case bottles are embossed or bear seals, often dated. Our examples are rarely identified in this manner, however, so that they can be dated only in a very general way. Those made prior to 1830 usually feature a flat, flared lip and less taper from top to bottom. Fragments of vessels showing these characteristics have been found at the Glastonbury, Connecticut, glass factory (active 1816–1827).

The containers that were made between 1830 and 1860 have an applied sloping collar and were often free-blown and shaped by use of a wooden paddle. In the earlier portion of this period many vessels show open pontils, like those from the preceding generation. In the final stage (1860–1900), cases were blown in a dip mold, unpontiled and of a generally standardized shape. They tended to have longer necks than earlier examples. The typical specimen from this period was formed in a ridged mold and is amber, a relatively standard color as is green. Less often encountered in this category are milk glass, aqua, and clear glass. While most case bottles are about a half gallon in capacity, they may be found in sizes from a half pint to several gallons, the larger examples being quite rare.

Although thought of today as gin bottles, these receptacles were used first for medicine and later for rum. Gin was not discovered until the mid-seventeenth century, so it is a relatively late comer to the field. Since certain wide-mouthed flared-lip cases from the early period are known, it may be assumed that these are early preserve or storage jars.

FIGURAL WHISKEYS

Prior to the passage of federal laws governing the manufacture and sale of alcoholic beverages, liquor—particularly forms such as rye and gin, which were inexpensive and easy to produce—was made throughout the

Opposite top: Clear glass figural whiskey in form of a pig. (Courtesy Burton Spiller)
Opposite bottom: Three wicker-covered demijohns. (Courtesy Staten Island Historical Society)

Below: Chestnut bottles in various shades of green, from New England, Pennsylvania, and the Midwest. (Courtesy Robert Anderson) *Opposite:* Detail of figural whiskey, bearded man in red amber glass. (Courtesy Burton Spiller)

United States. Nearly every community had one or more distilleries, and competition among producers was severe. At an early date, unusual containers were devised as a way of stimulating sales. Ornamental flasks, which are treated separately in this text, were the initial stage. Some of these date to the first decade of the nineteenth century. Then, before 1850, a variety of unusual figural containers emerged, many of them paralleling in form the medicinal bitters which, thanks to the efforts of prohibitionists, were the distillers' main competitors.

Perhaps the earliest major source of figural whiskey bottles was Bininger and Company of New York City. This family-owned grocery and dry goods business was established in New York prior to 1830 and continued to be active well into the 1880s. Its first containers were made in England, but it soon turned to domestic glass factories, which provided a remarkable range of unusual bottles, including barrels, clocks, jugs, and cannons. Three of the more spectacular examples are worthy of mention. The Bininger handled amphora and a wide-mouth vase are unique among early glass. The cannon-shaped golden amber container is similar to other bottles made in both the nineteenth and twentieth centuries.

Bininger also used a barrel-shaped container, as did several other liquor dealers. Its red amber Old Kentucky Reserve Bourbon is dated 1848/49, and the open pontil bears this period out. Of course, this piece must take a back seat to a rare and gorgeous peacock-blue barrel, which unfortunately does not carry any marking.

A number of dealers employed bottles in the shape of a pig. Found primarily in ordinary clear or amber glass, these vessels are most popular with collectors. In this chapter may be seen one such animal in clear glass,

53

marked "Something Good in a Hog's," followed by an embossed hand pointing toward the pig's tail. This ribald device appears on several different pig bottles. A second pig figural is known, fashioned of aqua glass and bearing the embossed name and address of what is probably a Louisville, Kentucky, saloon. Both these animals are mold-blown with hand-finished necks.

While it is unclear why the pig was so popular as a whiskey container, one may speculate that it related to his diet, which was corn, a major ingredient also of bourbon whiskey. There are also a few other animal figurals, best known of which is the milk glass Atterbury Duck, a well-shaped vessel that once held cordial.

Another popular figure—so popular, in fact, that it has been reproduced numerous times—is the E. G. Booz Old Cabin Whiskey. This container in the shape of a small house was blown in a full-size mold with an applied collar. It was first manufactured about 1860 for a Philadelphia merchant named Edmund Booz. Originals of this vessel, such as the one shown, are in amber glass, but it was later reproduced in milk glass, blue, green, purple, and yellow.

In the period 1880–1910 a series of spectacular molded figural bottles was manufactured. These have much more in common with their modern-day counterparts than with earlier bottles. They are primarily in milk or frosted glass or a combination of these and metal; and they are clearly intended to capitalize on popular or patriotic themes. Thus, one may see Grant's Tomb in milk glass, monumental figures of Columbus and the Statue of Liberty, both in milk glass and brass, and a frosted representation of Bob Fitzsimmons, the famous early prizefighter. All of these receptacles are composed of two or more parts, and they are rarely found in-

tact. As a result they are highly prized and quite expensive.

The frosted blue glass golfer shown is, perhaps, a bit later than the preceding examples but is certainly a most interesting figural. Like the others, it was probably used as a receptacle for cordial rather than one of the more common drinks. It appears that the majority of these bottles were identified by paper labels only, for despite the care with which they were made (and the likelihood that this resulted in a higher price for receptacle and contents), very few of them bear embossed identification.

There are only a few miniature figural liquors, most of which were probably intended to be given away as samples by distillers or saloons. A six-inch-high bottle in the shape of an ear of corn stoppered by another smaller ear with ground glass fitting was patented in 1891. It was made for the Elk's Whiskey Company and was produced in both clear and the much less common green

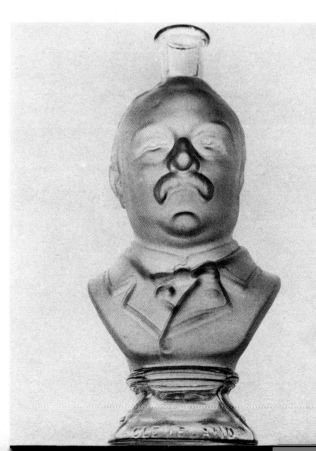

Right: Clear glass figural whiskey, bust of President Grover Cleveland. *Opposite:* Black milk glass figural whiskey, coachman in high hat. (Both, courtesy Burton Spiller)

vessel are particularly well done; and the pieces are by all standards most interesting even though made of clear glass. In shape, however, these flasks are undistinguishable from thousands of others, mostly unmarked, which were carried in the pockets or lunch boxes of workers all across the nation. This particular configuration is known, incidentally, as a "coffin flask," hopefully for the shape rather than the consequences of over-indulgence.

Smaller, half-pint variations might fit very neatly into a lady's purse. One of such containers carries the marking "JN Kline & Co's/Aromatic Digestive Cordial," indicating that women certainly might have felt the need of a nip on occasion. Much more common than these vessels are the clear or amber flasks marked simply "Picnic" and referred to, customarily, as picnic flasks. They were particularly popular in the Midwest in the early twentieth century and were traditionally carried for refreshment at Sunday outings and days of celebration. These smaller receptacles are commonly seen in clear, aqua, or amber glass, but are rare in other colors.

The collector of wine and spirits bottles may find his quarry in several areas, depending on his specialty. Those who seek the very early squat forms will find it necessary to buy from dealers at high prices and will have to content themselves, with rare exceptions, with European examples. Collectors of chestnuts, demijohns, and carboys, wine bottles of the later period, and case bottles have a wider field for exploration. All of these vessels may be found with dealers and at bottle shows or through publications. With the exception of chestnuts, they may also, on occasion, be dug up or discovered in ancient storage places. The same is true of handled whiskeys and the later decorated figural whiskeys, particularly the flasks.

glass. About the same time a miniature glass canteen was also distributed. Since some of these containers bear the embossed letters "G.A.R.," it is likely that they were made to serve as mementoes of an annual encampment of the veterans of the Union Army.

Directly related to the larger figural bottles, which are primarily a fifth or a quart in capacity, are pint and half-pint pocket flasks. These were sometimes true figurals, as in the case of the Bininger clock (title page); more often they were just heavily embossed vessels in a flat ovoid or coffin shape. Two interesting specimens are known to exist in the latter form. When William McKinley opposed William Jennings Bryan for the presidency in 1896, some unknown glasshouse produced identical pint flasks, one proclaiming "In McKinley We Trust," the other, "In Bryan We Trust." The likenesses of the candidates appearing in a medallion on each

4
Figured Flasks

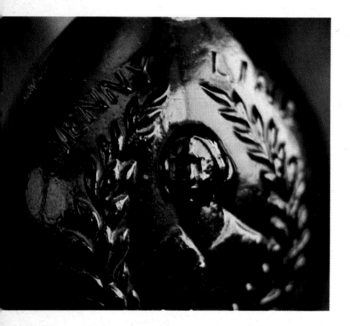

Above: Detail of calabash flask with embossed portrait of the singer Jenny Lind. *Opposite top:* Violin or scroll flasks. *Opposite bottom:* Early portrait or historical flasks. From left to right: emerald green, bust of Washington, with eagle on reverse; eagle on each side; sapphire blue, eagle, with Washington on reverse. (All, courtesy Burton Spiller)

The utilization of flat, more or less ovoid containers for the sale and transportation of liquor appears to be a custom long extant in the United States. These small bottles, typically a pint or half pint in capacity, occasionally ranging up to a quart, have been made and advertised here for at least two hundred years. They are known as flasks. One of the earliest references to such receptacles is a notice for the Newfoundland, New York, glassworks, which appeared in the *New York Gazette or Weekly Post Boy* of October 30, 1758. The proprietors advised the public "that any gentleman may be supply'd with . . . flasks or any sort of glass."

Nothing is known of the vessels made at Newfoundland. Other eighteenth-century flasks have survived, though. Henry William Stiegel's Manheim, Pennsylvania, glass factory (1765–1774) produced a wide variety of pattern-molded pieces in a somewhat bulbous form, with truncated neck and fire-polished lip. While these have been termed perfume, toilet, and pocket bottles, their specific use is uncertain. Their form, however, is fairly similar to that of later flasks.

In shape, at least, the prototype for nineteenth-century flasks appears at the New Bremen Glass Manufactory operated by John Frederick Amelung. This shop, in Frederick County, Maryland, was established in 1785. Eight years later one of the resident glassblowers blew a clear pint flask engraved with

the name of Francis Stenger, a glassmaker at an early New Jersey factory. This presentation piece is dated 1792 and may be regarded as one of the first examples of glass made to commemorate various trades, since the symbol of a bottle, trademark of the glassworker, appears on one side along with a Masonic symbol signifying Stenger's membership in that group. In its flat, semiovoid shape and plain lip this vessel is quite similar to later flasks, particularly those made in the period 1800–1825.

At East Hartford, Connecticut, as early as 1788, William and Elisha Pitkin developed a parallel form, the pocket bottle, blown in the Germanic half-post technique, with finely ribbed pattern-mold decoration in a swirl, vertical, or broken swirl configuration. The Pitkin flask, as it is commonly called, was an elongated flattened vessel with a short sheared neck. The methods by which it was produced were distinctly European. An initial gather of glass was redipped in the metal pot, thus covering the vessel with a second layer that did not extend the length of the first—hence the term "half-post." This second gather was patterned in a small dip mold: for vertical or swirled ribbing only a single insertion was required; for a double pattern of swirled and vertical ribbing (broken swirl), two insertions were necessary, with the swirled effect achieved by twisting or rotating the glass after the initial placement.

Despite the prevalence of the term "Pitkin" to describe this class of containers, excavation at other Eastern glasshouse sites has shown that they were manufactured at Coventry, Connecticut, and Keene, New Hampshire, as well as at East Hartford. New England examples appear primarily in various shades of amber and green.

The form spread also to the Midwest, where glassblowers trained in the Germanic tradition were making similar pieces at the Mantua, Kent, and Zanesville, Ohio, glassworks as well as in Charlestown, West Virginia, and New Geneva, Pennsylvania. Most of the Western specimens date to the first quarter of the last century. They are found in a wider range of colors than the Eastern bottles—brilliant aquamarines, greens, and ambers—and are, on the whole, squatter and more bulbous than their New England relatives. Since, however, none of the known Pitkins can be identified other than by general form or individual history, it is often difficult to assign a given example to an area, much less a specific glasshouse.

All of the previously discussed flasks were either free-blown or patterned in dip molds. A third method, which required using a full-size mold, was established in this country early in the nineteenth century. Such molds, generally composed of brass, cast iron, or pottery, had been known in the Near East from the time of the Roman Empire. They continued to be used throughout the Middle Ages and up until the eighteenth century, when the technique was largely abandoned except in the manufacture of simple square-section case bottles, medicines, and porters.

Around 1800 American glassmakers developed a new interest in such molds and began to use them to shape figured flasks intended as containers for rum, gin, or whiskey. These vessels, which clearly were advertising devices, bore various embossed scenes or figures. They were extremely popular with the public, and their manufacture continued well into the nineteenth century, with well-designed examples such as the Pike's Peak Flask being sold as late as 1875.

At present, the earliest of these containers is believed to be a green sunburst flask that was manufactured at the Pitkin works. On one side it bears an eagle, below which appear the initials "J.P.F.," for John P. Foster, who assumed the management of this shop in 1810. There are, however, a large number of other early pontiled flasks that might date to the first decade of the nineteenth century. Further excavations at glasshouse sites, particularly in the Northeast, may well establish prior examples.

Figured flasks have been arbitrarily divided into two classes. The first, termed historicals, generally encompasses embossments of presidents, national and international celebrities, patriotic emblems such as the flag or eagle, and insignia of societies, particularly the Masons. As a rule, one may say that the historical flasks embody a meaning or significance beyond themselves. The presidential examples, as an illustration, were often designed to attract voters to a candidate's cause by linking him to a prior respected holder of the same office, as in the well-known Washington-Taylor flasks.

A second group, pictorial flasks, includes

a wide variety of purely decorative motifs and devices, such as the sunburst, the scroll, or the cornucopia. These seem to have no meaning beyond the possibility that their attractive appearance might promote increased sales of both bottle and contents.

Prominent among the historicals are, as mentioned, those vessels that bear portrait busts of well-known personages. The majority were produced before 1850, and they include five presidents: George Washington (who appears on no less than sixty different flasks), John Q. Adams, Andrew Jackson, William Henry Harrison, and Zachary Taylor. Two specimens of the Washington flasks are illustrated here. One is a sapphire blue pint bearing on the reverse a portrait of Taylor, then a candidate for president. It was made at the Dyottville Glass Works in Philadelphia. There is a second Washington-Taylor flask, also from Dyottville. This one varies in design and is a claret or deep amethyst in hue.

Thomas W. Dyott, a bootblack who rose to become the owner of one of Pennsylvania's major bottle manufactories, produced a vast number of flasks in a wide range of colors. As an example, in the March 2, 1825, edition of the *Columbia Observer* he offered for sale "3,000 gross Washington and Eagle pint flasks, 3,000 gross Lafayette and Eagle pint flasks, 3,000 gross Dyott and Franklin pint flasks, 2,000 Ship Franklin and Agricultural pint flasks, 5,000 gross assorted Eagle pint flasks, 4,000 gross Eagle, Cornucopia and etc. half pints."

Though even in the case of Washington there was occasional dissent—for example, the nefarious toast of the early 1800s, "General George Washington: May tribute due his memory now be forgotten"—the father of his country seems to have been the only American political figure to attain unchallenged

Opposite top: Portrait flasks. From left to right: two Washington flasks, with Gen. Taylor on reverse; Summer-Winter flask. *Opposite bottom:* Sunburst flasks. *Top:* Pictorial flasks. From left to right: locomotive, inscribed "Success to the Railroad"; rare inverted cornucopia, eagle on reverse; Lafayette, DeWitt Clinton on reverse. (All, courtesy Burton Spiller) *Above:* Pictorial flask, Washington, with Taylor on reverse. (Courtesy Mrs. Robert Pattridge)

popularity on historical glass. John Quincy Adams and Andrew Jackson, as symbols of the patrician-proletarian schism that has haunted America even to our own day, employed the figured flasks as political weapons. Their supporters offered symbolic representations of the candidates filled with a "healing potion," in a deliberate attempt to curry favor with the electorate. At a time when a pint of whiskey cost only a few cents, it is readily understandable that such a method would find favor in all branches of political persuasion, with the exception of the Prohibition Party, of course.

Harrison, Taylor, and even Henry Clay, that perennial also-ran, appeared on figured flasks, but you did not need to be an aspirant for high office to obtain a place in this alcoholic hall of fame. Thomas Dyott, the Philadelphia glassmaker, saw fit to memorialize himself in this way, linking his own visage to that of Benjamin Franklin. New York's DeWitt Clinton was honored for his role in building the Erie Canal, and Maj. Samuel Ringgold of Maryland for his feats in the Mexican War. Examples of these flasks appear among the illustrations.

Clinton appears on a bottle that also bears the embossed likeness of the illustrious Lafayette. This dark green flask was made at and marked by the Coventry, Connecticut, Glass Factory Company. The Coventry shop, active from 1813 to 1850, made no less than two dozen different kinds of flasks. That these were both inexpensive and produced in great volume may be seen from existent company records. In 1846 the chemist Isaac Bull of Hartford was billed for eighty-one dozen pints at only thirty-one cents per dozen. Interestingly enough, half-pint flasks, of which he ordered thirty-eight dozen, cost more. They sold for thirty-seven and a half cents for twelve.

As an adopted son and Revolutionary War hero, Lafayette was often honored on historical flasks. When he returned to the United States for a final visit in 1824, fourteen different glass manufacturers commemorated the event with newly designed vessels. Another patriot, more charismatic than successful, was Louis Kossuth, who reached America in 1851 after fleeing Hungary following the collapse of the short-lived Republic there. Kossuth hoped to obtain this country's assistance in throwing off the yoke of the Austrian Empire, but although he was generally well received, both the populace and the government were opposed to intervention. The Hungarian revolutionary toured the country for a year and departed in 1852, leaving behind (among other things) a flask and three calabash bottles as mementoes.

It was not necessary, however, to be a political or military figure in order to obtain a place on the figural flasks. It was only necessary to be a celebrity. Thus, there is a pint bottle bearing the features of two different men, which has been known for many years as the Scott and Byron Flask. Whether the mold maker really intended to portray Sir Walter Scott and Lord Byron is a moot question, since there is no identifying lettering and only by the most generous standards can the portraits be said to resemble the originals. Moreover, most users of the vessels would have had at best only a hazy notion of who these illustrious foreigners were. In any case, these are but two of the many unidentified busts appearing on figured flasks. Some were no doubt meant to represent individuals well known at the time or possibly identified on attached paper labels. Others, perhaps, were purely decorative.

With the exception of the figure of Columbia—important less as a woman than as a national symbol—few women have graced the contours of these receptacles. Among those who did is Jenny Lind, a Swedish singer brought to this country by P. T. Barnum, the fabulous nineteenth-century showman and confidence man. Barnum deposited a guarantee of $187,500 to cover Lind's performances, an unheard-of amount in those days, and launched a massive publicity campaign to assure sell-out houses. The public and the glass manufacturers responded. Lind's tour was a financial and artistic triumph, and at least six glasshouses produced twelve different bottles bearing her portrait. Of these, nine were calabashes—long-necked bottles that became popular around 1850—and three were flasks, one pint and two quarts. A representative example is shown here.

The only other woman to grace a flask was Fanny Elssler, a European dancer and mime who toured this country from 1840 to 1842. Elssler made her American debut at New York's Park Theatre on May 14, 1840, and continued in triumph across the country. Sometime after her stay a pint aqua vessel appeared, bearing on one side the embossed figure of the dancer in costume for her role in the ballet *La Tarentule*. On the reverse appears a soldier. The embossments "Chapman" and "Balt. Md." on the flask make it likely that it was manufactured at the Maryland Glass Works, established at Baltimore in 1849 by John Lee Chapman.

Symbols as well as figures appeared on flasks. Among the former were many that had a direct relationship to the growth and expansion of the country. The period 1820–1840 witnessed a tremendous development in the agricultural and industrial sectors of the economy. The "American System," promoted with fervor by Henry Clay, relied on an elaborate system of protective tariffs to protect emerging native industries.

The great majority of those who bought the flasks and drank the whiskey were farmers, laborers, or small merchants, who knew from bitter experience the effects that cheap imported foreign goods had on their jobs and profits—particularly during the recession following the War of 1812. Consequently, they were quick to endorse tariffs, and flasks bearing symbols and phrases in support of American economic growth were widely made and sold.

Flowering trees, cornstalks or ears, sheaves of rye, cornucopias, and urns overflowing with the fruits of the land portrayed the richness of the developing country. Many of these are illustrated here, and it is not surprising that most such flasks bore on one side busts of founding fathers or those who later sought to take their places.

But agriculture and industry were both ultimately dependent on transportaion, for produce and goods had to reach a profitable market. This concern was reflected in the figured flasks. The first interstate road, the National Pike, was laid out from Washington, through Wheeling, West Virginia, and on eventually to Saint Louis. Because overland carriage was expensive and slow, better means of transportation were sought. On land, railroads were developed, at first employing extremely primitive horse-drawn carts running on wooden rails. These were replaced in due course by the steam engine and steel rails. The initial horse and cart was pictured on several flasks, which bore the hopeful phrase, "Success to the Railroad." Two variations on this theme were produced at Coventry, Connecticut, and Mount Vernon, New York. Crudely modeled representations of the first steam engine also appear on a few flasks. Several forms are believed to have been made at the Lancaster Glass Works, in Lancaster, New York.

Right: Pictorial flasks. From left to right: green, eagle, embossed on reverse "Louisville Glass Works"; aqua, trotting horse, embossed "Flora Temple"; green amber, anchor, with cabin on reverse. *Below:* Calabash flasks. From left to right: golden amber, bust of Louis Kossuth, with sailing ship on reverse; blue, anchor and sheaf of wheat, with "Baltimore Glass Works" on reverse; green, bust of Jenny Lind, with view of glass factory on reverse. (All, courtesy Burton Spiller)

While rails came to be dominant in the second half of the nineteenth century, water transportation was always of great importance. Flatboats and barges used the rivers, and the completion of the Erie Canal in 1825 (heralded by the Clinton-Lafayette Flask) marked the beginning of an intensive period of canal construction. Ships of various sorts appeared on the flasks as well as anchors and slogans about "sailors' rights." Many of the ships depicted were warships or in some other way only remotely connected to commerce; but in one case, at least, the link to business was clear. The rare American System Flask depicted a side-wheel steamboat on one side and a sheaf of wheat on the other— a juxtaposition clearly designed to illustrate the necessity for a system of water transportation between market and producer. Appropriately enough, this flask is embossed "The American System."

The symbols of national identity, the flag and eagle, appeared regularly, often on the reverse of pictorial flasks, as though it were important then, as now, to remind the citizens that national political figures really had national interests at heart. The eagle was particularly popular, appearing on more than one hundred flasks prior to 1850 and half as many thereafter. While it was manufactured in the standard pint and half-pint sizes, the eagle was also found on quarts. The Willington Glass Company of West Willington, Connecticut, offered one of the few examples that bore a maker's mark. This flask, which was embossed "West Willington, Conn.," was a standard item in the company's stock. During the period 1866–1870, it sold at $4.37 to $7.00 per gross for the half pint, $6.00 to $9.00 for the pint, and $8.00 to $12.00 for the quart.

Eagles were frequently combined with unusual motifs, such as the morning glory vine, floral medallions, grapes, trees, lyres,

stags, and agricultural implements. That these are all to some extent related to farming and farm production is, perhaps, no coincidence, since the eagle flask was most popular during the period of westward expansion and rural development.

The flag is seen on a much smaller number of containers, but among these are some extremely choice examples, including the very rare milk glass flask made by Coffin and Hay of Hammonton, New Jersey, and embossed "For Our Country." Also known is another unusual flag flask, this one from an early Pittsburgh glasshouse. The banner is combined with a large cider keg and the phrase "Hard Cider," symbolic of the Harrison campaign of 1840.

A final group, usually classified among the historical flasks, are the Masonics. These vessels, of which some forty different types are known, are all of substantial age. The earliest, made primarily at the Marlboro Street works in Keene, New Hampshire, date to before 1820; the last specimens were blown around 1830.

The Masons were and are a secret society of some prominence. Lafayette and Andrew Jackson were members, and their profiles are found in conjunction with Masonic paraphernalia on several flasks. It is difficult to determine why these vessels were so popular, but it is not hard to understand why this popularity came to an end. In 1826, William Morgan, a member of a western New York chapter of the society, disappeared after threatening to publish the secret rites and passwords of his group. Though several explanations of his fate were published and a body found on the shore of Lake Ontario was claimed to be his, Morgan was never seen again dead or alive. Public outrage at his disappearance culminated in violent anti-

Masonic activity, including formation of a political party dubbed the Anti-Masonics, which was able to command a substantial number of votes throughout the 1830s.

As a consequence, Masonic emblems of every type vanished from public view. The flasks that had been produced remained, however; and among these are some of the loveliest examples in the entire field. A wide variety of colors—greens, blues, purples, amethysts, ambers, and grays—are found, as well as clear glass. Various combinations and arrangements of Masonic devices appear, either alone or in conjunction with historical busts or other forms. Among the Masonics shown in this book is an aqua-colored specimen that may well be unique. It bears an eagle on one side and the Masonic gate and paraphernalia on the other.

So-called pictorial flasks, those with purely decorative motifs, form a minority of the total group available to collectors. In many cases, however, they are among the most interesting. Foremost in terms of size and color variations are the scroll or violin flasks. These pear-shaped vessels were made in half-pint, pint, quart, two-and-one-half quart, and gallon sizes, the last an extremely unusual size for a flask. The color range in this category is extraordinary, being exceeded by no other group of nineteenth-century bottles. Amber, green, blue, citron, amethyst, blue moonstone, gray, clear black, and glass ap-

Pictorial flasks. From left to right: amber,
embossed bowl of fruit, with Baltimore Monument
on reverse; golden amber, embossed ear of corn,
with Baltimore Monument on reverse; aqua, rare
embossed bunch of grapes. (Courtesy Burton Spiller)

pear in all their hues. Similarly, as to molds, over eighty different ones have so far been identified. It would be possible for a collector to build a major collection in this area alone. The three scrolls illustrated in this chapter—emerald green, amber, and light green—all vary slightly in form and come from different glass factories. They reflect in a small way the great variety available.

Sunburst flasks form another interesting subspecies. These are for the most part quite early, the products of New York and New Hampshire shops. Some thirty different examples are known, all in pint or half-pint size, with ambers and greens predominating.

While scrolls and sunbursts are examples of pure form, the bulk of the pictorial flasks illustrate an array of objects and creatures, many of which have the quality of cartoon characters illustrating popular activities, figures, or songs of the day. As such they are valuable to us as representations of nineteenth-century mores and morals. The bulk of these vessels were produced in the period 1850–1890, when mold quality was declining, and they are seldom as attractive as earlier flasks, but they are often more interesting. For example, a flask from the 1870s is embossed with a girlish figure riding an early bicycle and the words "Not for Joe," a phrase taken from a popular song of the period. Another widely circulated bottle—one that appeared in several variations—was the so-called Pike's Peak Flask. This appeared at the time of the 1859 Colorado gold rush and reflected the western movement of prospectors heading for the gold strike located in the area around Pike's Peak. The most common form shows, on one side, a bearded prospector striding along with walking stick and backpack, while on the reverse, another—or perhaps the same—man is seen shooting a deer. This scene is related to the design of the

much rarer Great Western Flask. On this unusual container a buckskin-clad mountain man is pictured in detail, while on the back appears his quarry, a wide-antlered buck.

The Pike's Peak flasks continued to be made some years after the excitement had gone out of the '59 strike, at least into the 1870s. An 1872 price list published by the Pittsburgh Glass Works offers the vessels in quarter-pint, half-pint, pint, and quart sizes at $10.00, $12.00, $16.00, and $24.00 per gross respectively.

There are other genre scenes to be found on American flasks. The unpopular Civil War draft act inspired a receptacle bearing the figure of a man walking in haste, with coattails flying and hat off, while a bayoneted rifle points menacingly in his direction. Any doubt as to the meaning of this tableau is resolved by the single word appearing in a cartoonlike balloon issuing from the figure's mouth. That word is "Drafted."

Hunting and fishing as popular pastimes of the common man were also memorialized in glass. An uncommon flask of the late period portrays a hunter, probably seeking ducks—a small boat is seen near at hand—with his two dogs. More often found is the Hunter-Fisherman Calabash, in which each side is adorned with an appropriately garbed and outfitted sportsman. The Indian, as prototype of the outdoorsman, also finds his place here. Two rather similar flasks are known, each bearing the embossed representation of a crowned or feathered brave aiming his bow at a bird in flight. A tiny dog watches from a distance. Both bottles were probably made in the Pittsburgh area, as one of them is marked "Cuninghams & Co./Pittsburg, Pa."

Animals were also rather popular as decorative devices in their own right. Dogs, as mentioned, appear several times in connection with hunting scenes. Deer are also found, not only as parts of larger compositions but also independently, as on the aquamarine pint and half-pint flasks made by Coffin and Hay at Hammonton, New Jersey. In these an antlered buck is seen on the obverse accompanied by the phrase "Good Game," while, perhaps symbolic of his fate, a weeping willow tree appears on the reverse.

A crude duck or goose adorns one of the Traveler's Companion flasks (the embossed phrase on these bottles relates, perhaps, to whiskey's ability to make a journey pass more quickly); while another duck is the key to one of the more humorous genre flasks. In this case the phrase "Will You Take a Drink" is balanced against the words "Will A . . . Swim," with the figure of the bird taking the place of the appropriate word.

Horses, too, were important, not only for field work and transportation but as a source of sport and gambling. While there are several flasks and calabashes on which a standing horse is seen, the most interesting example is the Flora Temple Calabash, which is illustrated on page 64. Flora Temple was a famous trotting horse that established an impressive record for the mile. Her time and the name of the glasshouse that made the bottle—Spring Gardens Glass Works, Baltimore—are blown into the vessel. It dates to the 1850s.

A few rather general, symbolic pictorials also exist. The famous Summer-Winter Flask shows a tree on each side, in one case in full leaf, in the other bare to winter's winds. Stars, usually ,of the eight-pointed type, appear either alone or in conjunction with other motifs. The Lockport and Lancaster, New York, glassworks particularly employed this device on their Traveler's Companion line of flasks. In this category may also be included the cornucopia and urn bottles, though their obvious relationship to American agricultural development may also justify their placement in the historical category.

No other area can compare with flasks in terms of the scope and variety available to collectors. Over four hundred different types appeared before 1850, and several hundred more are known from the remainder of the century. The finest examples, in terms of quality of artistic representation, were created in the first period. After 1850, mold makers seem to have lost much of their skill and vitality; portrait flasks nearly vanished, and standard designs such as the eagle and the urn became sketchy and uninspired. The cartoon flasks that replaced the earlier forms were interesting more for their subject matter than for their skill of execution. Few were really well done, often even lacking central placement on the available surface.

The collector seeking to amass a substantial number of historical and pictorial flasks will have little trouble obtaining the more common specimens. These vessels have been collected for decades, and most antiques and bottle dealers stock them. They are, however, quite expensive. Even the most ordinary cost $35, while rare examples range into the hundreds or even thousands of dollars. Prices tend to be standardized and well known in the trade, so that "sleepers" are seldom encountered. While it is true that occasional specimens still show up in dumps or storage spaces, most bottle diggers will labor for years without finding one. After all, these receptacles were intended to be decorative, and most were preserved from the time they were first purchased. It should also be noted that counterfeits exist, most notably the Czechoslovakian Jenny Lind Calabash of the early 1900s, and should be watched for. They can generally be distinguished on the basis of color and glass quality.

Unique and unrecorded example of a Masonic pictorial flask; aqua, gate and emblems, with eagle on reverse. (Courtesy Burton Spiller)

5
Decanters & Bar Bottles

Above: Clear flint glass bar bottles, marked "Linquist Private Stock" and "Whiskey."
Opposite: Clear flint glass bar bottles, marked "Duncan McIntosh's Highland Whisky" and "Cortwright Rye." (All, courtesy Jim Wetzel)

Decanters and bar bottles differ from most other glass containers in that they are not normally used for the transportation of liquid but for its storage and in some cases its sale. As early as 1670 slender, ovoid, shouldered vessels were being used for the storage of fruit juices. Soon after 1700 the well-to-do began to employ clear glass containers for wine and various whiskeys. These receptacles were either of the slender form or of a squatter barrel shape.

Traditionally, wine, like fruit juice, was transported in wooden kegs or barrels in the bottoms of which a sediment settled. Decanting, the process of transferring a liquid from one container to another without disturbing this unwanted deposit, was desirable not only because it improved the clarity and taste of the beverage but also because the fluid was distinctly more attractive in the clear flint glass vessels into which it was poured.

The earliest decanters were unadorned, though like their successors they boasted matching glass stoppers. Decoration—particularly engraving or etching—became popular in the late eighteenth century, and large numbers of decorated receptacles were imported into this country. There was a native industry as well. The 1752 inventory of the possessions of Caspar Wistar, the New Jersey glassmaker, listed ten dozen and three pint and half-pint decanters valued at £5 12s. 9p.

And naturally Henry William Stiegel also made decanters. His account books indicate that between 1769 and 1770 he had on hand or disposed of 1,968 plain quart decanters, 6,374 pints, and 3,319 half pints. The term "plain" no doubt refers to the fact that these vessels were free-blown and, perhaps, undecorated. The record, however, also makes mention of 923 molded quart decanters, an indication that Stiegel was employing pattern molds similar to those he used in making flasks. Stiegel turned out decanters in capacities much greater than those popular with later glasshouses—his notice of July 6, 1772, in the *Pennsylvania Packet* mentions "four, three, two, and one quart decanters with stoppers, pint and half pint, ditto." Most such containers found today are in pint, fifth, and quart sizes.

There are numerous other references to pre-1800 American decanter production. The little-known Philadelphia Glass Works advertised them in 1775, and notices appearing in the *Maryland Journal and Baltimore Advertiser* for May 16, 1789, indicate that John Frederick Amelung had also entered the field. Certain clear glass containers bearing copper wheel engravings have been attributed to his works.

Soon after 1800, mold-blown decanters gained ascendency. At Keene, New Hampshire, the Marlboro Street Glass Works (1815–1841) produced a variety of such vessels shaped in a three-piece mold. They were made of flint glass in pint and quart capacities and in a variety of colors from clear to various shades of green and even cobalt. An example in the crystal flint appears here.

Mold-blown examples were often further decorated by cutting. The *Norwich Courier* of Norwich, Connecticut, noted on July 31, 1816, that the Boston Glass Manufactory was offering "FLINT GLASS AS DECANT-ERS, WINES, TUMBLERS, & MOULDED and CUT into all the varied forms of taste and fashion." Perhaps the leading firm in cut glass was Bakewell and Page of Pittsburgh, Pennsylvania. Established in 1808, this company was the United States' first mass producer of cut-glass specialties. By 1825, the year it received the "Reward For The Best Cut Glass Pair Of Decanters" at the annual exhibition of Philadelphia's Franklin Institute, it was dominant in the field. In 1817 Bakewell and Page manufactured a matching set of decanters for President Monroe, of which it was said that they were "a splendid equippage of glass consisting of a full set of decanters . . . exhibiting a brilliant specimen of Double Flint, engraved and cut by Jardelle, in which this able artist has displayed his best manner, and the Arms of the United States on each piece have fine effect."

Similar ware was made at the Mantua Glass Company, Mantua, Ohio, around 1822–1829; at Kent, Ohio, also in the 1820s; and at Deming Jarves's New England Glass Company in East Cambridge, Massachusetts. In 1819, the latter offered for sale, via the *Boston Commercial Gazette,* "18 packages Prussian Quart Decanters and 5 packages pint decanters; 4 packages ring quart and pint decanters." The Prussian decanters referred to are those in which clear blown flint glass was engraved for decorative effect in the manner of Amelung. The "ring" decanters mentioned are molded vessels with one or more protruding rings about the neck above the shoulder. These were both decorative and practical, as they tended to assure a firmer grasp on the bottle. An example of a ringed decanter, also termed a "pully ring bottle," appears here. It is in a style that had appeared at the turn of the last century and remained popular until 1850.

Decanters shaped in three-piece molds continued to be much in demand throughout the first half of the nineteenth century. A great many patterns are known, among the most famous of which are the ornate forms produced at the Boston and Sandwich Glass Company during the 1830s and 1840s. One of these, in the shell and rib pattern, is pictured here. Among the more unusual vessels attributed to Sandwich are four-inch miniatures, which were perfect imitations of their larger cousins.

Around 1850, presses began to be employed in the making of tablewares, and during the Victorian era pressed-glass decanters were extremely popular. The Cape Cod Glass Company (1858–1882) at Sandwich, Massachusetts, was advertising quart bar and table decanters with glass or slide tops in 1863. They were available in several patterns including those called Cape Cod, Utica Mirror, and Gaines. Pressed glass was intended to imitate the more expensive cut types, and like them it was often lavishly decorated. The examples made at Cape Cod Glass were truly spectacular, with decanters often engraved and gilded as well as cut.

Another late-nineteenth-century development was Bohemian glass, a form of cased glass in which two or three layers of colored metal were laid over a clear base. The glassmaker then cut through the layers of colored glass, exposing the colorless interior in a multitude of picturesque designs. The New England Glass Company produced a substantial number of decanters decorated in this style during the period 1850–1870. Blue, red, and green were the favorite hues employed in this manner, and engraving further added to the extravagance of the vessels.

Bohemian glass was a sensation when it first appeared. Referring to the wares made at the New England Glass Company, the *Philadelphia Bulletin* of June 16, 1852, proclaimed that

> the variety and beauty of the articles manufactured there would scarcely be credited for one not a visitor; but we assure our readers that we saw many works that could not be surpassed in Bohemia or any place else in Europe. The various processes by which the different colors and the rich gilding are produced, we are not prepared to describe; but they are produced in these works in the utmost perfection.

Decanters have been made for so long and in so many different designs that the collector has a wide selection from which to choose. They have been decorated with molded, applied, cut, enameled, engraved, etched, gilded, flashed, and stained motifs. Most of the motifs are purely decorative and nonrepresentational. Some, however, have a historic or personal reference. Thus, there are vessels with engraved patriotic slogans like "Free Trade," the coats of arms of the United States and various individual states, eagles, sailing vessels, Masonic symbols, and the like. On a more prosaic level, it has long been customary to blow, etch, or engrave upon the container some denomination of its intended contents, such as "Gin," "Rum," "Wine," and so on.

Since at least 1800, decanters have been available with matching metal stands, generally with an attached handle for ease in holding. The Camden, New Jersey, *Courant* for May 29, 1820, noted that the New England Glass Company was offering for sale "rich plated, 3 and 4 bottles liquor stands, 1 superior gold plated, 4 bottles, silver mounted and eagle handle."

While most decanters were manufactured from clear flint glass, other colors were available. Amethyst, red, ruby, cobalt, and light blue as well as various shades of green may be found. In size these bottles range from four-inch miniatures to at least four quarts.

Bar bottles may initially be differentiated from decanters in that they do not have a flanged lip and are clearly designed to receive a cork rather than a glass stopper. They first appear in newspaper references soon after 1800. The December 26, 1816, edition of the *Connecticut Courant* made some mention of "quart bottle decanters," which it described as lacking a flange and as not being ground for stoppers. These were blown three-mold vessels, often in the same forms as decanters; they had a greater variety of shapes, however. Some were extremely bulbous throwbacks to an earlier era in design. Others were square or cylindrical editions of decanters, distinguished only by their collared necks. Such were the "1 package moulded liquor bottles" that the New England Glass Company offered in its notice appearing in the *Boston Commercial Gazette* of March 27, 1820.

It is unclear what function these containers served in the early 1800s and in what way, if any, they were distinguished from decanters. By the last decade of the century, though, a clear line of difference had emerged. Bar bottles were by then primarily intended for use in the serving rooms of public houses, taverns, hotels, and the like. They were specifically referred to as bar bottles and were clearly segregated from decanters.

Blown and pressed-glass bar bottles of this period were often blown or engraved

Clear flint glass bar bottles, marked "H" and "Sunny Glen." (Courtesy Jim Wetzel)

with a notation as to their contents, just like decanters. However, such words as "Rum" or "Gin" did not provide the drinker with any indication as to the source of the beverage, merely its type. Then, around 1900, increased competition between liquor distillers and an awareness of the value of publicity encouraged manufacturers to offer the tavern owners free bar bottles from which to disperse bulk whiskey—which in those days was largely purchased by the keg or barrel. These receptacles were primarily made from clear flint glass and bore the enameled or gilded name of the distiller whose product they contained. Since they were used behind the bar, they came to be called back bar bottles. As may be seen from the examples illustrated, they came in a much greater number of shapes than did the traditional bar bottle. Some were cylindrical shouldered containers much like a modern fifth or gallon; others were bulbous enough to match the early decanters, or heavy and squat like ships' decanters of the same period. A few even bore the flanged lip and glass stopper associated with traditional decanters, though they were technically not such, as they all showed the manufacturer's or product name common to back bar bottles.

Most people who collect bar bottles must be content with clear glass, made more interesting by the various brand names found thereon. There are a few colored glass containers, most notably in amber and in cobalt, as well as interesting examples with lithographed labels set into a recess and covered with a glass panel, as in the case of barber bottles. The lithos generally include a brand name and the portrait of an attractive woman. In a few cases, instead of a lithograph, the woman's picture may be hand-painted, occasionally in a daring pose or state of undress. Such decoration is in high demand, and these bottles are at a premium.

Collectors interested in decanters and bar bottles have a large selection from which to choose. On the other hand, most examples are now in collections or the hands of dealers. A few common bar bottles, particularly from the late period—up to 1920, when they were driven from the market by federal regulations—may be found in dumps or storage places, but both types have always been regarded as decorative bottles and so carefully preserved. Prices for the bar bottles are at present relatively higher, though choice decanters have always commanded good figures. It should be noted that the large numbers of imported Irish and English decanters make this an area where specific knowledge of the characteristics associated with the native American product is particularly important.

6
Proprietary Medicine Bottles

The number and variety of proprietary medicine bottles is so great that they form the bulk of most collections. No one knows for how long physicians and other medical practitioners have been bottling and selling nostrums to the unsuspecting public, but in this country alone the time span exceeds two hundred years. During this period thousands of bottles have appeared, each labeled or embossed with the name of a different remedy. The field is so extensive that many collectors specialize in a single subarea, concentrating, for example, on cures or balms.

The first proprietary medicines that were sold in America were imported from England, where "patents of royal favor" were issued to makers of such concoctions as early as 1710. While the term "patent medicine" has been used in this country since the colonial period, it is not an accurate designation. There is no record of a King's Patent covering a nostrum developed here; and few patents covering medicines were issued by the United States Patent Office after its establishment in 1790. Since the Patent Office required full public disclosure as to contents, it was often against the best interests of manufacturers to apply for a patent. After all, you wouldn't want the public to know that your remedy, like Dr. Townsend's Sarsaparilla, was composed of nothing more than sassafras bark, molasses, and cheap rye whiskey. What the proprietor chose to do instead was

Proprietary medicine bottles. *Above:* Miner's Damiana and Celery Compound for the Cure of All Nervous Diseases. *Opposite:* From left to right: aqua, Clemen's Indian Tonic; clear, Pure Family Nectar; aqua, Blodgett's Persian Balm. (All, courtesy Burton Spiller)

to coin a catchy trade name—Spark's Perfect Health or Spiller's Golden Balsam—and register it with the Patent Office. With judicious advertising the name would become the product and could easily be protected under the trademark regulations.

As long ago as the mid-1700s remedies were being promoted in a manner strikingly like that employed by modern advertisers. Thus, the *Pennsylvania Chronicle* of August 7, 1769, hailed the Pectoral Cordial Emulsion as "a medicine safe and powerful against any hectic complaints, which it very soon relieves; and, it being taken . . . according to directions, totally extirpates the disorder."

Quite a few eighteenth-century patent medicine notices are known; in fact, they constitute the majority of all newspaper advertising for the period. At a time when products were far more expensive than human labor—the selling price of Pectoral Cordial Emulsion was equivalent to a day's wages —nostrum sellers joined silversmiths, cabinet makers, and grocers in dominating the written media.

The first of these "medicines" were sold in unmarked vials or in bottles with paper labels. It soon became evident, however, that a popular remedy would have its imitators; and to guard against this, mold-blown receptacles bearing the producer's name appeared. At present the earliest known reference to such a bottle is an ad for Dr. Robertson's Family Medicines in the *Pittsburgh Gazette* of February 16, 1810, where it is noted that each bottle of the Robertson remedies had the proprietor's name embossed on it. The falsification problem continued, however, with imitators going so far as to employ workers with names identical to those of the makers of well-known compounds, in order to justify the use of similar trade names. Outraged manufacturers took their competitors to court

and even resorted to notifying the public of such duplicity through notices such as the following, from the *Connecticut Courant* of April 18, 1836:

Caution—Beware of Counterfeiters: Every Purchaser who values health will observe that each genuine bottle we sell has Anderson's Cough Drops, prepared by J. Mellen, stamped in the glass and that each of the directions are signed in writing J. A. Mellen's. Examine before you purchase, as there are a number of spurious kinds in market, similar in appearance but very different in their effects.

There are very few embossed proprietary medicines that can be traced to the years before 1800. Robert Turlington's Balsam of Life, an English-made remedy sold in this country from 1744 until the end of the nineteenth century, may be one. Some of its early pontiled, pear-shaped vessels may date from the eighteenth century, but we cannot be sure. Between 1800 and 1840, however, a substantial number of embossed pontiled medicines were produced. Some of them were in colored glass—rich greens, blues, yellows, and reds, all of which command premium prices among the few collectors fortunate enough to acquire them. An exceptional group of these bottles is on display at one of the historic buildings at Richmondtown Restoration, Staten Island, New York. The cobalt Elmer's Medicated Soda, illustrated, is one of five known examples, and the amber Dr. Townsend's Sarsaparilla is an early example of the remarkable concoction previously mentioned.

Aqua proprietary medicine and household bottles. From left to right: Dr. Porter, New York; University Free Medicine, Philadelphia; Ballard's Hair Dye, N.Y.; John C. Baker & Co., Druggists. (Courtesy Joan and Larry Kindler)

A Dr. James Jackson of Dansville, New York, stated after only a few years in practice that he knew over nine hundred patients who confessed to draining from three to fifteen bottles each of Townsend's potion during the time they were his patients—whether from extraordinary faith or because of its high alcoholic content, we do not know.

Since medicine bottles, particularly early ones, rarely bear the mark of the bottle factory where they were blown, it is difficult to ascertain their origins. The business was so extensive that it is likely that most glasshouses produced them. As early as 1826 George Brinley and Company, glassmakers of Boston, Massachusetts, was advertising its willingness to sell "Patent Bottles stamped and lettered at a small extra expense." In the 1850s, Weeks and Gilson of South Stoddard, New Hampshire, turned out containers for Seaver's Nerve and Joint Liniment and for Opoldeldoc; while at New London, the Fort Trumbull Glass Works blew bottles for Dr. Ford's Pectoral Syrup and Perry Davis's famous Pain Killer. Of course, many of the larger proprietors had their bottles made at more than one factory, so that in most cases one can only speculate as to their origin.

While use of narcotics and alcohol as ingredients certainly furthered the remedy business, as did the advertising, the manufacturers could never have succeeded without the credulity of its customers. Many people clearly believed in the efficacy of the potions they consumed. But that's not all that surprising. Until the 1700s, medical treatment was largely of the folk variety, consisting of large doses of witchcraft leavened with medicinal herbs that had been proved capable of relieving certain symptoms. As the practice of medicine developed, doctors—or those who represented themselves as such, for examinations and license laws did not exist—followed a

bewildering variety of disciplines. Homeopathic, eclectic, botanic, bleeding, and calomel schools arose to compete vociferously with each other. Their fees were high for the time and the results extremely uncertain. Many people lived far from any medical practitioner at all.

Following the American Revolution, a national devotion to public education led to a literacy rate far above that in most areas of the world. As the new readers became accustomed to reading the local newspapers springing up throughout the country, they also became habituated to curing their ills with the patent medicines advertised in their pages. At a very early period, testimonials from relieved and grateful users were used as a device to further nostrum sales. For example, on July 23, 1810, John Owens of Baltimore wrote to the *Delaware Statesman* in praise of one such mixture:

> Messers Michael Lee & Co.;
>
> I think it is my duty to inform you that from experience I am convinced your ague and fever drops is an effective remedy. My little son was violently afflicted with ague and fevers—the advice and assistance of an able physician failed. I was advised to try the country air—which also failed—and it appeared to all that saw him impossible for him to recover, when Mr. George May advised me to try Lee's Ague & Fever Drops (observing that they had cured him). A bottle was procured and given according to directions which effected a speedy cure and he has not had a return thereof since.

Such declarations became a common feature of proprietary medicine promotion, the typical newspaper ad consisting of several paragraphs extolling the virtues of the medi-

Proprietary medicine bottle, Old Dr. Townsend's Sarsaparilla, in rare blue glass. (Courtesy Helene and Barry Shatoff)

cation followed by up to a dozen short letters from satisfied customers. The more prominent the writer, the more likely his letter would be to induce sales, and it was not long before national figures began to appear in promotional literature. Gen. Horatio Gates urged every soldier going to the front to take Nuxated Iron. The same substance was credited by Jess Willard with being responsible for his victory over mighty Jack Johnson. Buffalo Bill Cody endorsed Kickapoo Indian Sagwa, Lillian Russell tried Carboline for the hair, and Sarah Bernhardt spoke highly of both Duffy's Pure Malt Whiskey and Paine's Celery Compound.

As the nineteenth century progressed, the patent medicine business prospered. Two general lines were always offered: "specifics," for curing a single disease, and "cures," for a multitude of illnesses, which in some cases might extend to nearly all the afflictions known to man. Thus, a notice for Dr. Moore's Essence of Life, which appeared in the *Connecticut Courant* for March 13, 1805, recommended the potion "for Consumption, Difficult breathing, Quinsy, Phthific Spitting of Blood, Flatulency, Fits and Hypochondriac afflictions." At a later date, Green Mountain Vegetable Ointment was offered as a cure for ague, bronchitis, sore throat, quinsy, croup, felons, ringworm, burns, piles, shingles, erysipelas, salt rheum, cholic, scrofula, rheumatism, gout, and inflammations of the eyes and bowels. And all this for a dollar!

With several thousand different remedies on the market, many claiming to cure the same diseases, competition among sellers became severe. Testimonials were no longer enough. New gimmicks had to be devised, and they were. By the 1850s the Indian had been driven far enough west that he had become for most Americans a curiosity rather than a source of terror. Taking advantage of this interest, medical entrepreneurs turned out a raft of native cures—Indian Compound of Honey Boneset, Dr. Morse's Indian Root Pills, Indian Salve, Dr. Kilmer's Indian Cough Cure, and so on. Two of the less common examples from the early part of this period are Masta's Indian Balsam and Clemen's Indian Tonic (shown page 77). The tactic was to picture the Indian as a natural physician healing himself with secret root and herb remedies. The producer of the nostrum would then represent himself as a public-spirited soul who had learned these formulas, generally in return for some kindness to the native, and was now offering them to the public. Betsy Masten, originator of Aunt Betsy's Green Ointment, claimed to have received the compound from an aged Mohawk squaw whom she had given food and shelter.

Capitalizing on growing interest in distant shores and exotic people, manufacturers also brought forth a variety of oriental and Mideastern cures and even one from the icy North. The virtues of Hutching's Compound Syrup of Iceland Moss were claimed to have been "first discovered by their effects on the hardy, long-lived and sagacious Rein-Deer which derives its principle nourishment from the Iceland Moss, and whose milk becomes so highly embued with its balsamic virtues that it is used with the greatest confidence as a sovereign remedy by the inhabitants of all those countries" (*Connecticut Courant,* May 9, 1836).

Rare colored pontiled proprietary medicines. From the left: Front: Chapman's Genuine; Elmer's Medicated Soda; C. Brinckerhoff's Health Restorative; C. Heimstreet, Troy, N.Y.; Kimball's Jaundice Bitters; Mrs. E. Kidder Dysentery Cordial. Back: Dr. Perkins' Syrup; ABC Myers, Rock Rose; Swaim's Panacea; Hyatt's Infallible Balsam; Dr. Townsend's Sarsaparilla. (Courtesy William J. Geisz)

Nor did the proprietors wait for customers to come to them. Salesmen known as "medicine men" traveled across the land bringing the blessings of the cure to every village and crossroads. The so-called low-pitch medicine men usually traveled by foot or public transportation, carrying their wares in a large suitcase that doubled as a sales table. They stood on street corners and relied on light banter and a hard sell to bring in business. The "high-pitch" salesman was much more aristocratic. He traveled in a brightly decorated wagon and addressed the crowd from it or from a rented stage, often preceding his sales pitch with a variety show or other entertainment. These medicine shows were often the only theatrical productions available in rural areas and were always well attended. They were so popular that the Kickapoo Medicine Company at one time had no less than seventy-five separate acts touring the country. Trade cards, give-away programs, and flyer mailings at reduced postal rates also served to keep the public informed of the virtues of the many remedies available.

All this effort was not without its rewards. Many of the manufacturers became rich, very rich. Dr. David Jayne of Philadelphia, discoverer of Jayne's Vermifuge (once described as a muddy brown liquid in an oval green bottle), Jayne's Sanative Pills, and Jayne's Alterative, owned several blocks of buildings in his native city and built himself a $300,000 mansion with silver doorknobs, French glass, and his daughters' faces sculptured on each mantel. At his death he left an estate of three million dollars.

The three unusual bottles seen on page 92–93 are from the H. H. Warner Company of Rochester, New York. A former safe salesman whose full name was Hulbert Harrington Warner, the proprietor began in 1879 to issue a line of remedies developed by a Dr.

Craig, one of which had allegedly cured Warner of Bright's disease. Warner's products numbered twenty different varieties, many packaged in containers of unusual shapes—an uncommon thing in the proprietary field, where most bottles were rather ordinary. So great were his sales that Warner opened branch offices in London, Melbourne, Frankfort, Prague, and other distant cities. He lived in a huge Victorian Gothic mansion, owned a yacht, sponsored a baseball team, and even built a private observatory.

Frequently the one who profited was not the originator of the panacea. Dr. S. Andral Kilmer of Binghamton, New York, developed a line of tonics, pills, and ointments that he was unable to merchandise. His nephew, Willis Sharpe Kilmer, obtained the formulas for a pittance and used them to build a fortune. After first eliminating the elderly doctor and a brother from the business, Willis introduced a massive advertising campaign particularly directed at the bellwether of the line, Swamp Root the Great Kidney Specific. Sales soared and within a few years Kilmer could devote most of his time to horses—including a Kentucky Derby winner—travel, and cultural activities. He founded a newspaper and became an avid art collector and the owner of several estates, a yacht, and numerous automobiles. When he died in 1940 his family was left an estate valued at between ten and fifteen million dollars.

By 1905 domestic patent medicine consumption had reached 365 million bottles per annum. In the next year sales totaled eighty million dollars. Then the bubble burst. *Colliers* magazine had initiated a series of articles on nostrums in the fall of 1905. The serial, written by the well-known Samuel Hopkins Adams, was well researched and carefully documented. Much to the public's surprise, it revealed that most proprietary medicines

Aqua pontiled proprietary medicines. From the left: Front: Clickin's Sugar-Coated Vegetable Purgative Pills; Turlington's Balsam; Jewett's Liniment for Headache. Back: unmarked; Stephen Sweet's Infallible Liniment; Doctor S. Herman's Olosanian. (Courtesy J. and L. Kindler)

Colored pontiled proprietary medicines. From left to right: Dr. Guysott's Compound Extract of Yellow Dock; Bartine's Lotion; Smith's Green Mountain Renovator; C. W. Merchant, Chemist. (Courtesy Burton Spiller)

contained alcohol—in fact, 240 brands on the market had such a high alcoholic content as to require a liquor license for their sale—and that some were laced with such health restoratives as arsenic, opium, and morphine. The resultant outcry led to the passage in 1907 of the Pure Food and Drug Act, which required strict accountability from makers as to contents and advertising quality. Though the law was far from perfect and had to be strengthened at a later date, it had an immediate effect on the remedy business. Many nostrums were driven from the market, and those that remained had to alter their ingredients or tone down their advertising to such an extent that they became pale specters of their former selves. The great advances made in medicine during the twentieth century further reduced the field available to these concoctions; and though one can still

find patent medicines on drugstore shelves, particularly in poor or rural areas, their role is greatly diminished.

Medicine bottles for the most part are not unusual either in form or color. The majority range in size from three-inch miniatures to a one-quart capacity. They are made in varying shades of aqua or amber glass. While round or oval containers are not un-

Opposite: Aqua pontiled proprietary medicines. From left to right: Hunt's Liniment; Davis Vegetable Pain Killer; R.R.R. Radway; Johnson's American Anodyne Liniment. (Courtesy Helene and Barry Shatoff) *Above:* Amber proprietary medicine, Spark's Perfect Health for Kidney & Liver Diseases. (Courtesy Burton Spiller)

common, a square or rectangular shouldered bottle with a long neck is the major type.

All proprietaries originally bore labels, and most were also embossed with the maker's name; very few had embossed decorative designs. The quart golden amber William Radam's Microbe Killer is a great favorite with collectors, because of its vivid depiction of a battle between Death, whose scythe lies shattered at his feet, and the club-wielding man of science. Less common is the amber Miner's Damiana and Celery Compound, which seems to illustrate a housewife at the local grocery store. The bust that appears on the front of Spark's Perfect Health may be a portrait of the proprietor, or possibly an as-yet-untreated patient! Another popular container is the lovely emerald green Pine Tree Cordial. The pine tree on its face is one of the better examples of folk art in this area.

Proprietary medicines offer a fertile field to the collector. Many bottles, such as Pinkhams, Radways, Warners, or Pierces, were made in such great numbers that they are readily obtainable in all sections of the United States. These more common examples often can be purchased for a dollar or less each. Moreover, almost any untouched attic or cellar will yield a few specimens; and they are sometimes so common in dumps that diggers leave dozens of duplicates on the site. In fact, a major problem with this area is space—any serious collector soon finds his treasures running into the hundreds. As a result most people now specialize in only a single area, such as tonics, liniments, or cures. For the more sophisticated there are the pontiled bottles, particularly the colored ones, or the very few decorative receptacles, like the Warner's Safe Cure and the Pine Tree Cordial. Whatever your choice, proprietaries are historically fascinating and offer a fertile area of research. There is much yet to be uncovered.

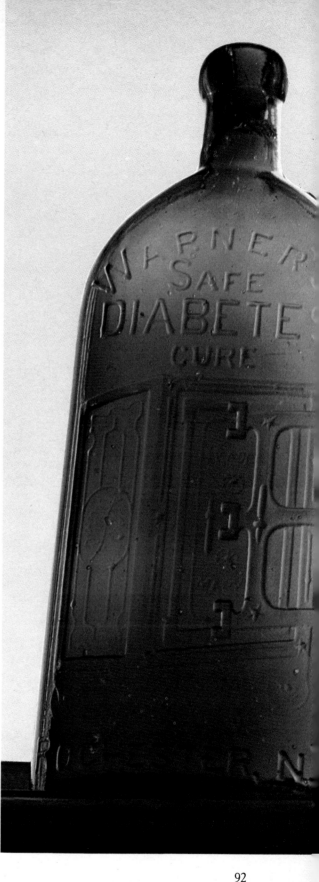

Proprietary medicines. From left to right:
amber, Warner's Safe Diabetes Cure; rare green,
Tippecanoe for Dyspepsia; amber, Log Cabin
Sarsaparilla. (Courtesy Burton Spiller)

7
Bitters Bottles

Above: Pontiled bitters bottles. From left to right: aqua, Phoenix Bitters; green, Phoenix Bitters; aqua, W. L. Richardson's Bitters. *Opposite:* Labeled bitters, Dr. H. S. Flint & Co.'s Celebrated Quaker Bitters. (All, courtesy Burton Spiller)

The term "bitters" is generally taken to apply to an infusion of herbs, particularly quinine and others with a similar acrid taste. Such substances have been used for many years to alleviate stomach disorders. Technically, then, bitters are proprietary medicines, and they have always been dealt with as such under federal law.

Bottle collectors, however, have chosen to segregate this class of remedies and to collect them as an independent group like flasks or barber bottles. And, indeed, bitters lend themselves to this approach. There are over a thousand known varieties; and unlike most patent medicine receptacles, which are rather ordinary in form and color, bitters bottles appear in spectacular shapes and colors.

The first commercial bitters were bottled on the European continent in the seventeenth century. They consisted of various herbal mixtures steeped in water, generally without the addition of alcohol. In England, however, the mixtures were employed in quite a different way. There, during the reign of George II (1727–1760), the government, in an effort to control the wholesale drunkenness that had enveloped the working class, levied a heavy tax on gin, which was the cheap spirits used by most people. Not to be denied a lucrative market, the liquor manufacturers simply steeped a few harsh-tasting herbs in gin and called the resulting concoction "gripe," "coltick water," or most com-

Two 1860 Plantation Bitters bottles, green and amber. (Courtesy Burton Spiller)

monly, "bitters." This deception was an immediate success and established a pattern for later, like-minded producers.

Before the American Revolution, British authorities also derived substantial revenue from a tax levied on the rum and gin consumed in the Colonies. Bitters were consequently laced with rum to avoid the impact of the tax. However, we should not discount the faith many people had in the medicinal value of such mixtures. At the conclusion of the struggle for freedom, alcohol taxes were removed, not to be restored until the 1860s; but bitters did not disappear from the market. Notices recommending their good properties appeared in many early newspapers: "To Invalids. Dr. Richardson of South Reading, Massachusetts, in compliance with the solicitations of his numerous friends has consented to offer the public his celebrated VEGETABLE BITTERS . . . which he has used in his practice in Boston and its vicinity for more than thirty years" (*Connecticut Courant,* February 1, 1836). Richardson's was claimed to be a specific remedy for "dyspepsia, sensation of weight, eructions, wandering pains, flatulency, etc."

Apparently a good number of people suffered from these ailments, for Dr. Richardson's concoction remained popular for decades. One of his early pontiled bottles, dating from the period of this ad, is shown. It would be interesting to know if the alcoholic content of the beverage remained constant over the years. In 1882, an analysis revealed Richardson's to be 59.14 percent alcohol, or 118.28 proof, a very high figure even for bitters.

Certainly, the popularity of most of these remedies owed not a little to their ability to provide a warm glow. Whiskey was for many years regarded as an essential by most settlers, women as well as men. However, the accidents and antisocial behavior produced by excessive drinking led at an early date to the formation of prohibition organizations. As far back as 1785, Dr. Benjamin Rush's *Inquiry into the Effects of Ardent Spirits on the Human Mind and Body* had prompted an outcry against imbibing; and as the nineteenth century progressed, opposition, particularly among women, became stronger. Many a farmer or artisan, finding that his spouse was strongly against rum or gin, turned with gratitude to the healing bitters. Yet it would be naive to think that the women were always deceived. Bottle diggers frequently find bitters containers under barns, hidden in stone fences, and buried in old outhouses, mute evidence of the never-ending struggle between couples over "the staff of life."

It should not be assumed, however, that all American bitters had an alcoholic base. Dr. J. Walker of San Francisco made a tidy fortune from a nonalcoholic bitters. He had it both ways—first, by cutting costs through leaving out the booze; second, by appealing to the temperance market, which shunned the products of his fellow entrepreneurs:

CALIFORNIA VINEGAR BITTERS
Millions bear witness to their wonderful curative effects. They are not a vile fancy drink made of poor rum, whiskey, proof spirits and refuse liquor, doctored, spiced and sweetened to please the taste, called tonics, appetizers, restorers, etc., which lead the tippler on to drunkenness and ruin, but are a true medicine made from natural roots and herbs of California. . . . They are a great blood purifier and a life-giving principle. For female complaints, whether in young or old, married or single, at the dawn of womanhood or turn of life, these tonic bitters have no equal.
J. Walker, Proprietor (Middletown, Delaware, *Transcript,* January 4, 1873)

Actually, Walker's compound was composed of herbs, nitric acid, and pond water; but it did the trick, at least for him. He lived to be nearly a hundred years old, rich and a pillar of temperance.

The bitters business was given a boost in 1862 when the federal government, burdened by wartime expenses, abandoned its reliance on customs duties and property taxes for an extensive system of sales taxes. Both alcohol and proprietary medicines were subject to these levies, but the former was taxed at a considerably higher rate. As a result, more consumers found themselves subject to the afflictions bitters were supposed to cure, and there was a substantial increase in the number of manufacturers and variety of brands. When one considers the alcoholic content of these "medicines," the injustice of the tax system and the cleverness of the imbibers becomes evident. Most whiskey is 80 to 90 proof. Tests conducted in 1882 by Dr. H. W. Vaughn, the Rhode Island Assayer, revealed that many of the popular bitters equaled or exceeded these standards. For example, Hostetter's Bitters were 86 proof, Baker's 81 proof, Atwood's 80 proof, and Drake's Plantation 76 proof.

As temperance groups developed, so did the bitters trade. The establishment of the Women's Christian Temperance Union in 1874 and the Anti-Saloon League in 1895 did not really displease the manufacturers, since most of the "drys" remained singularly unaware of the alcoholic content concealed in these remedies. However, Samuel Hopkins Adams's articles on proprietary medicines and the subsequent passage of the Pure Food and Drug Act struck hard at the business. Once they were required to reveal how much ardent spirits they had tucked away in their products, the manufacturers became fair game for the women with hatchets, and the estab-lishment of national prohibition in 1920 destroyed the business. The repeal in 1933 of the Prohibition amendment did not revive the dormant factories; so that unlike some other proprietary medicines, bitters have now passed from the scene.

The bitters manufacturers sold their wares in much the same manner as the producers of other proprietary medicines. They used the newspapers, billboards, sandwich men, flyers, posters, trade cards, traveling salesmen, and, of course, medicine shows. They were also quite as willing to appropriate the names of the famous, with or without permission. Lily Langtry voluntarily—and, no doubt, for some compensation—promoted Brown's Iron Bitters. On the other hand, Sulphur Bitters "honored" Mrs. Grover Cleveland with a trade card bearing her picture, though quite without consent.

Deceptive advertising, the bane of all medicine men, plagued this field as well. Thus, the makers of San Sevain Wine Bitters found it necessary to alert the public to impostors in the following manner: "In ordering wine bitters be sure you ask for the San Sevain Wine Bitters manufactured by Mercado & Scully, San Francisco, for inferior kinds are often substituted. Observe the yellow labels and see that the name of Mercado & Scully is on the wrapper, label and stamp" (*Santa Cruz Times*, November 16, 1867). The resentment of a successful proprietor when faced with those who would trade on his good name and reputation knew no bounds. When speaking of such a scoundrel, one bitters king advised his patrons to "look at him and you will see 'Penitentiary' written in his countenance; that is his destiny, sooner or later."

Bitters bottles may be divided into several distinct categories, and some collectors

Labeled bitters bottles. From left to right: aqua, Gates' Life of Man Bitters; amber, Dr. Petzold's German Bitters; aqua, Vegetable Bilious Bitters. (Courtesy Burton Spiller)

limit themselves to only one or two of them. The earliest containers are pontil-scarred and usually square or rectangular, with tapered corners. Some round and eight-sided vessels are also known; they come in aqua, amber, or some shade of green and may be dated to the first half of the nineteenth century. Among the relatively few bottles in this class are Richardson's, Phoenix, and the early At-wood's Bitters, and iron-pontiled specimens, such as the triangular-shaped Caldwell's Herb Bitters. Illustrations of these first bottles appear in the text.

There are also a large number of figurals, including cabin and barrel shapes. The former are particularly popular; three choice examples—Holtzerman's Patent Stomach Bitters, Kelly's Old Cabin Bitters, and the 1860 Plantation Bitters—are shown. The last, in an interesting green, is a bottle with an unusual history. The remedy it contained was developed just prior to the Civil War by Col. P. H. Drake and was promoted by use of the phrase "S.T. 1860 X," which appeared on the container and in advertising material. Drake's men also painted the cryptogram on barns, fences, and billboards, on high rocks and cliffs, and even on a prominent headland near Niagara Falls. While some people maintained that the mysterious notation stood for "started trade in 1860 with ten dollars capital," the proprietor always contended that it was meaningless, just a bit of doggerel to incite curiosity and increase sales.

Barrels are also a great favorite. Over a dozen different forms exist, and acquiring all of them presents a real challenge. Color is particularly noticeable in this group. The hues range from emerald green (Greeley's Bourbon Bitters) through puce (Old Sachem Bitters and Wigwam Tonic) to various shades of yellow (Hall's Bitters), amber, and black glass (Bourbon Whiskey Bitters). We may assume that the form itself is related, like bottles in other categories, to the barrel symbolism of the Harrison presidential campaign of 1840.

There are also vessels in the shape of animals, the best known being the pig and the fish. Both Berkshire and Suffolk Bitters were sold in an amber container representing a kneeling pig. These bottles are related in both form and content to the pig whiskeys previously discussed. The fish-shaped bottle is amber also, and once contained Fish Bitters. An almost identical container was used in the twentieth century for the sale of cod liver oil.

Human figures are of interest to many collectors. Simmons' Centennial Bitters was packaged in an aqua bust of George Washington, while both H. Pwarazyn and the maker of Brown's Bitters favored a rather majestic figure of an Indian maiden, which was known appropriately enough as the Indian Queen.

In addition to these categories, there are a great many odd and unique shapes, such as lighthouses (Panacea Bitters), ears of corn (National Bitters), drums (McKeever's Army Bitters), clocks, cannons, and horseshoes. The range of colors is also extensive, including milk glass, blue, and amethyst in addition to those mentioned for barrel bitters.

Like their counterparts in the field of proprietary medicines, the purveyors of bitters were ambitious men, and many found fortune in the trade. One of them was Dr. H. S. Flint of Providence, Rhode Island, who cynically capitalized on the well-respected and well-known integrity of the religious group known as Quakers. He sent out pitchmen dressed in the fashion of the Society of Friends, who hustled the customers with Quaker phrasings and mannerisms, addressing all as "Brother" or "Friend" while offering most unfriendly advice and commodities. Illustrated here is a rare example of Quaker Bitters with the original label, showing a Quaker holding out a bottle of the remedy and featuring Flint's catchy password, "Try this and thou shalt be benefitted."

Flint was not a Quaker, but another successful bitters magnate was. Asa T. Soule of Rochester, New York, retained the Society's traditional business acumen while abandoning its ethical standards and parlayed Hop Bitters, "the invalid's friend and hope," into a tidy million. Among his playthings, once fortune was secure, was a baseball team, the Hop Bitters Nine, whose members were dosed before each game with generous amounts of the owner's remedy. Remarkably versatile as it was, the panacea was also recommended to the distaff side of the family. An almanac issued by the company advised that "Ladies need Hop Bitters monthly" and pointed out that the remedy saved expensive doctors' bills.

Perhaps greatest of all these businessmen were David Hostetter and George Smith, who merchandised a formula developed by Dr. Jacob Hostetter, David's father. A gigantic advertising campaign was the key to the success of Hostetter's Bitters. The proprietors not only offered to cure known ailments, they invented new ones; and they vigorously attacked all other remedies and treatments. A sample of their approach may be garnered from the following notice placed in the *Connecticut Courant* of July 31, 1868:

Some people think that chronic Dyspepsia may be cured by diet and exercise alone. This is a mistake. The stomach must be stimulated and regulated and the liver and the discharging organs put in good

101

Amber figural bitters, The Fish Bitters.
(Courtesy Helene and Barry Shatoff)

working order before a cure can be effected. Such is the operation of Hostetter's Bitters.

> They tone the stomach
> Set the liver right
> And put the stomach
> in such a healthful plight
> That good digestion
> Waits on appetite.

The monstrous cynicism of these merchants is almost beyond belief. On the one hand, they blandly assured the public that Hostetter's was "an unadulterated vegetable essence medicated solely with herbs and roots acknowledged perfectly harmless . . . even to children of delicate constitutions." On the other, at the beginning of the Civil War, they offered it to the government as a stimulant to soldiers before battle. Since the army had abolished the liquor ration in 1832, this offer was quickly taken up, and box cars of bitters followed the Union Army to the front. The recommended dosage of "half a wineglass on the eve of an engagement" was no doubt beneficial, since at the time, Hostetter's was 94 proof. The Confederacy countered with its own invigorant, Southern Bitters, which sponsors claimed would enable their forces to "throw off that general lassitude . . . resulting from our long hot summers." The eventual outcome of the conflict mirrored the fates of the two remedies. Hostetter's went on to fame, Southern Bitters expired with the Confederacy.

The Hostetter empire lasted well into the twentieth century, with sales at times surpassing a million dollars a year. Before he died in 1888—of a liver ailment—David Hostetter had constructed his own railroad and owned several factories, oil wells, and coal mines.

It is usually quite difficult to determine which bottle manufacturers made which bitters bottles. The glasshouses seldom blew their own names into the containers; and only occasionally did their advertisements or price lists mention the companies for which they were producing bottles. It is known that Hostetter had many bottles made in the Pittsburgh glass factories and that the Willington Glass Works of West Willington, Connecticut, was manufacturing containers for Kissingers and S & N Bitters during the third quarter of the nineteenth century. A surviving price list reveals that the company was charging $10.50 per gross for Kissingers in the pint size, while S & N pints went for $12.00 per gross in the same size. Also, Kimball's Jaundice Bitters were bottled in vessels produced at the South Stoddard, New Hampshire, glassworks during the period 1850–1873.

Collecting bitters is interesting and challenging. There are many embossed bottles, particularly common brands like Atwood's or Hostetter's, which can be obtained for a dollar or two. For others, in plain aqua or amber, the price increases with rarity. Figurals or containers in unusual colors, on the other hand, are very expensive. A substantial number of brands were identified only by label, and previously unknown variations in this category appear rather frequently. Because of a general prejudice against unembossed bottles, these seldom command the much higher price their rarity would seem to warrant.

Bitters show up fairly often in digs and in old buildings; but rarer types are best sought for at bottle shows and through the pages of bottle and antiques publications. It is not difficult to acquire a group of several dozen of the more common bitters; but the choice specimens have been collected for many years, and the competition for them is fairly heavy.

Amber bitters. From left to right: Wahoo &
Calisaya Bitters; Romaine's Crimean Bitters;
Niagara Bitters. (Courtesy Burton Spiller)

8
Beer Bottles

Above: Beer bottles. At left, aqua, embossed "Washington Brewery Company"; at right, clear glass, embossed "The George Bechtel Brewing Company." *Opposite:* Amber beer bottles. At left, Rochester Brewing Company; at right, from the Rochester Glass Works. (All, courtesy B. Spiller)

Beer may well be the oldest alcoholic beverage. It was brewed in prehistoric times and has been found sealed in ancient Egyptian tombs. Throughout the medieval period families customarily brewed their own, a custom that was brought to this continent by the first settlers. In fact, it is said that the scant water supplies aboard the Mayflower were replaced on occasion by the stronger drink.

In any case, even the earliest American settlements had breweries. The first were established at Roanoke, Virginia, in 1587 and at New York City in 1612. There can be little doubt that what these shops produced was not our modern beer but most likely ale or porter, a thick, dark brown malt liquor having an alcoholic content of 8 percent as opposed to the 3 or 4 percent found in modern brews.

For many years beer was transported in and sold from hardwood kegs or barrels, usually made of oak. Since beer in direct contact with wood takes on an unpleasant taste, the kegs were lined with pine pitch, which is tasteless and is not soluble in the brew. As late as 1850, most beer was sold in taverns or inns for consumption on the premises. If taken home, it was usually carried in a pot or bucket furnished by the customer. Early advertisements, therefore, often refer not to bottled beer but to the product in bulk. For example, in 1836, Weeks and

Pomeroy of Hartford, Connecticut, advertised "Hookers Cream Ale in Barrels, Half Barrels and Kegs...fresh from the Springfield Brewery, for sale and delivered at home price" (*Connecticut Courant,* October 15, 1836).

Such beer as was bottled appears to have first been sold in stoneware bottles with wired-down cork tops, or in heavy black glass bottles similar in form and size to the later mineral water containers. These vessels were known as junk bottles.

As early as about 1790, the Pitkin Glass Works in East Hartford, Connecticut, was advertising "Junk Bottles, suitable for bottling Porter." The type was widely made in other New England shops, including that of John Mather (ca. 1805–1820), also in East Hartford, and at the Boston Glass Bottle Manufacturing Company.

It appears that sometime around 1820, the term "junk bottle" fell into disuse, and the vessel came to be referred to as a porter bottle. Thus, by 1829 the New England Glass Bottle Company was advertising "three hundred gross best patent Porter bottles." In the pint size these sold for $7.50 per gross; quarts were a dollar more for the same quantity.

No junk or early porter bottles bearing the name of a brewery or distributor have been located, and it is possible that none was ever made—particularly since the receptacles were regularly used for cider, liquor, and other beverages as well as porter. There are, however, a few such bottles that bear, embossed on the base, the mark of the New England Glass Bottle Company (ca. 1825–1842). Like most other junk bottles, they have an open pontil. It is likely that containers of this sort were used by Manhattan's Greenwich Street Brewery at the time it placed the following notice:

GREENWICH-STREET BREWERY— JOHN NOBLE & CO.

Acquaint the public that their bottled porter is ready for immediate use. . . . Captains of vessels sailing from this port will find the above article worthy of their attention—particular care shall be paid to its being put up in such a manner as to become ripe in rotation, which will not only render it better but prevent breaking. All possible attention shall be paid to orders from any part of the continent. Nothing shall be added in recommendation of this PORTER—it might with justice be supposed to call in question the judgment and good sense of their customers, for after all it is their opinions that must decide upon its real value.

(*The Daily American*, June 11, 1802)

It seems that taverns as well as breweries regularly bottled their own brew, particularly in the earlier days. An advertisement placed in the *Delaware Statesman* of June 24, 1812, by one Eli Lamborn advised the public that he had opened a "bottling cellar" beneath his tavern, where porter, ale, and cider could be obtained by the dozen bottles or otherwise.

Sometime around 1850 mold-blown embossed bottles appeared. These were pint or half-pint containers with improved pontils and resembled in shape and color mineral water bottles of the same period. They were marked ale or porter, not beer, a term that does not seem to have been used on bottles until the 1870s.

One such bottle, a squat green vessel, is embossed "D. L. Ormsby/New York" on one side and "Philadelphia/XX/Porter & Ale/Union Glass Works" on the reverse. The Union Glass Works was active at New London, Connecticut, around 1860 and was

Clear glass beer bottles. From left to right:
Eckstein Brewing Company; miniature G. B. Seely's
Son; Henry Freiman's Bavarian Lager Bier.
(Courtesy Robert Anderson)

Above: Squat beer bottle, Bahr & Krasman Weiss Beer. (Courtesy R. Anderson) *Opposite:* Colored beer bottles. At left, light amber Anheuser, Busch Brewing Co.; at right, green pontiled early beer bottle, embossed "Phila. Porter & Ale."

known to use the emerald-hued glass found in this receptacle. Another green glass container with a similar improved or iron pontil is shown in this chapter. It is marked simply "Phila/Porter & Ale" and was quite possibly made at that city's Dyottville Glass Works, which sold large numbers of porter bottles during the 1850s and 1860s.

Like their predecessors, the squat bottles employed a cork closure, which was secured by wrapping wire about the neck under the protruding collar, then binding it across the cork. These receptacles are by no means common. Interestingly enough, the majority

found seem to have been manufactured of the rich green glass, though amber may also be found. The half-pint ale mold mentioned among the effects of the Westford Glass Company at the time of its bankruptcy in 1865 was, no doubt, designed to produce a vessel in this form. In 1870, the Willington Glass Company of West Willington, Connecticut, was selling half-pint porters at $4.00 to $7.50 per gross, depending on quality. It also made pint ales and pint and quart porters.

In the 1870s a new and very different container was developed. This was about ten inches high and had a blob top. It is interesting to note that though earlier and later brewers preferred a dark shade of glass, in the belief that it protected the brew, these bottles were most often of clear glass. Many were plain cylinders, but enough—perhaps 10 percent—were embossed in various ways to create an interesting field for collectors. As may be seen in the pictures (p. 104), a variety of figures and symbols was employed. The bust of Washington and a spread eagle on the Washington Brewing Company container are well done, a reflection of the use of patriotic motifs so common in the last century. The George Bechtel warrior, on the other hand, is clearly an allegorical figure. This bottle, incidentally, bears an intact example of the Lightning Stopper, which was invented in 1875 by Charles de Quillfeldt. This closure gradually replaced the cork on soda and beer bottles and remained popular with brewers until superseded by the crown closure after 1891.

A very few bottlers adopted a torpedo-shaped receptacle similar to those popular with manufacturers of carbonated drinks. The purpose of this form was to prevent the bottle from being placed upright, a condition in which the cork might dry out and shrink, leading to loss of the contents. One of these vessels, from Gleason's Brewery in Rochester, New York, is shown. They must be regarded as rare.

While the ten-inch cylindrical container was standard for many years before and after 1900, variations are known. The squat Bahr and Krasman pint on page 108 is one example. More interesting is the miniature, only three inches high, offered as a sample by the Seely bottling works.

Not all manufacturers adopted clear glass, and after 1900 most containers again assumed a darker hue. Amber is, accordingly, the most often encountered color; a few others are known as well. Aqua is fairly common, and there is one cobalt blue beer. It once contained "Liquid Bread—A Pure Extract of Malt." By any other name it was still just beer. Without doubt, the least-seen color in these vessels is yellow. A bottle of this color is known, which bears the embossed name of an old Staten Island, New York, brewing company, Rubsam and Horrman, and is thought to be unique.

Late nineteenth- and early twentieth-century beer bottles are fairly easy to come by. Great quantities, including some nicely embossed specimens, are regularly uncovered in the course of excavations by bottle diggers. A large number of cobalt Liquid Bread containers were found a few years ago during reconstruction of portions of a West Coast community. Dealers are also showing more interest in an area that until a few years ago was relatively unexploited by collectors. The earlier, improved pontil, Ale and Lager bottles are harder to locate, however, and one often must employ advertisements and word of mouth to acquire them. The field in general is still one where the beginning collector can accumulate a nice grouping without a major financial expenditure.

Beer bottles. From left to right: Family Ale
& Porter, A. & L. Lawrence; Rochester Brew Co.;
rare torpedo-shaped F. Gleason, Rochester; E.
H. Nelson Bottling Works. (Courtesy Burton Spiller)

9
Mineral &
Soda Water Bottles

Above: Mineral waters. From left to right: light green Congress Water; green Saratoga A Congress Water; rare wide-mouthed bottle embossed "Saratoga, N.Y." (Courtesy Robert Pattridge)
Opposite: Clear glass soda water bottle, G. B. Seely's Son, 319-331 West 15th Street, New York. (Courtesy Robert Anderson)

Mineral water may generally be defined as water that has been naturally or artificially impregnated with mineral salts or gases. When carbon dioxide is added to this fluid, it becomes carbonated, the fizzing, bubbly reaction associated with present-day soda pop. Natural mineral water—which is embued with mineral salts leached out of the soil through the action of ground water—has been known for thousands of years. Hippocrates wrote a treatise on its properties in 400 B.C.; and in A.D. 77, the historian Pliny discussed the great mineral springs of Europe, including in his list several that are still active.

It has long been believed—and there is some present-day medical theory to support the idea—that mineral water has curative powers. Early explorers on this continent showed a definite interest in mineral springs and recorded them as major finds on their travels. There can be little doubt, for example, that the "fountain of youth" sought by Ponce de Leon in Florida was a mineral spring. The Indians knew of many such springs and often informed settlers of their locations. As mineral springs are widely distributed across the United States, most sections of the country have had their mineral water craze. This usually began with stories of miraculous cures —often reported, of course, by the proprietor of the spring—followed by an increasing

number of visitors, which in turn led to the construction of hotels and other recreational facilities and the bottling of the waters for distribution to other, less fortunate areas.

At an early date many springs were discovered in the northeastern United States, particularly in New York. A large complex of artesian springs exists at Saratoga, New York, in the foothills of the Adirondack Mountains. In 1761, Sir William Johnson, a major colonial military figure and landowner, visited one of these known as the High Rock Spring. Though he expressed interest in the future of the spa, Johnson did not claim the waters, the first owner of record being a Dutch farmer named Rip Van Dorn. Even before the American Revolution, visitors began to frequent the springs at Saratoga, and crude log lodges were erected at the site in 1771 and 1774. By 1783 four different springs were known—High Rock, Red, President, and Flat Rock—and interest was sufficient to justify building a road from the settlement of Fish Creek. The constructor of this path, Gen. Philip Schuyler of Revolutionary War fame, built a home near Red Spring that he used as a summer residence.

It is not known when the Saratoga waters—or indeed any American mineral waters—were first sold in containers. It is said that the product of Jackson's Spa in Boston was first offered in bottles as early as 1767; and sometime around 1800 the Washington Lithia Well at Ballston Spa, a few miles south of Saratoga, was the source of the first bottled mineral water produced in New York State. The Ballston spring was an attraction until the 1850s, and a later receptacle from there marked "Washington Lithia Well/Ballston Spa/N.Y." is illustrated here.

Saratoga was the dominant Eastern center throughout most of the nineteenth century. Several dozen springs existed there, including the following: Aetna, Champion, Chrystal, Columbian, Congress, Eureka, Excelsior, Flat Rock, Geyser, Glaceier, Hathorn, Hamilton, High Rock, Leland, Paradise, President, Putnam, Quaker, Red, Saratoga "A," Saratoga Vichy, Seltzer, Star, Triton, Union, United States, Washington, and White Sulphur. Since more than half these springs prospered sufficiently to justify bottles embossed with their names, a collector can accumulate a sizable group by concentrating on Saratoga alone.

It should be noted that while some of these springs, such as the spectacular Champion Spouting Spring, were artesian—that is, those with water flowing or boiling to the surface—the majority were drilled wells.

Saratoga water was being bottled as early as the 1820s by the New York City firm of Lynch and Clark. An extremely scarce pontiled amber quart bearing the embossed mark "Lynch & Clark/New York" has been collected. It dates from approximately 1826. Business at the spas was increased through circulation of a popular book of the 1840s, Dr. Milo L. North's *Saratoga Waters, or the Invalid at Saratoga*. Like all such successful ventures, the spas depended greatly on newspaper advertising to spread the word. Notices like the following one from the *Connecticut Courant* of May 15, 1840, appeared in many newspapers:

FRESH CONGRESS WATER
A fresh supply (bottled within 10 days expressly for the subscriber) this day received and for sale at the sign of the good Samaritan
W. Brown, Boston
481 Washington Street

Green mineral water bottles from Saratoga, N.Y. From left to right: Star Spring Co.; Hotchkiss' Sons C; High Rock Springs; Hotchkiss' Sons E. (Courtesy Robert Pattridge)

A few months later the same paper carried advertisements for waters of the Congress, Iodine, Pavilion, and Fountain springs. All could be obtained by the bottle, dozen or gross.

By 1850 mineral water was big business in Saratoga County. Hotels for the devotees had been built at Saratoga Springs as well as the nearby watering places of Ballston Spa and Round Lake. The Congress and Empire Springs alone were so active as to justify their own glass factory. In 1844 the Mount Vernon Glass Company, which had been established in Oneida County, New York, in 1810, transferred its operations to Mount Pleasant, only ten miles from Saratoga. The company had found the timber resources in the western county to be seriously depleted; by moving east, it was able not only to tap the great woodlands of the Adirondacks but also to find a readymade customer in the mineral water business. The Saratoga Mountain Glass Works, as it came to be called, had not previously made mineral water containers, but in the next twenty years millions of such bottles went down the plank road linking the glasshouse and Saratoga Village. In 1850 alone, over seven million bottles were made for the spas, with the Congress and Empire bottling plant taking no less than a million of them. In 1865 the glassworks was sold to that company and transferred to Saratoga in a sector known as Congressville. It continued to operate there until 1890, and during this period a vast number of bottles for mineral water was manufactured.

Most of the bottles made at this factory are in the thick-walled, high-shouldered, sloping-collar form traditionally associated with the mineral-water trade. An interesting exception is the rare wide-mouthed jar marked "Saratoga, N.Y." which is illustrated here. This latter type of vessel, though generally considered a mineral, may more likely have been a blacking bottle. Blacking bottles are known to have been made at the Saratoga Mountain Glass Works, and the wide-mouth form would have been ill-suited for mineral water.

It should be noted that Congress and Empire bottles were also made at the Willington Glass Works in West Willington, Connecticut; a one-pint size was sold there at $10.00 per gross in 1866. Star and High Rock Spring containers were produced in New Hampshire at the South Stoddard Glass Company during the same period.

Though the major focus was on Saratoga, New York had many other mineral springs. In the western Adirondacks there were spas at Massena and Booneville, while directly east across the mountains was the Adirondack Spring at Westport. There was the Sharon Sulphur Spring in the Mohawk Valley, and, farther west, the Syracuse Spring and the famous acid waters at Batavia and Alabama. The latter, known as the Oak Orchard Acid Spring for its location on Oak Orchard Creek, was a major source of bottled waters in the late nineteenth century. Examples of vessels used in the distribution of these mineral waters are shown.

New England also had its share of spas. One of the most famous was the Poland Springs located in the Maine town of the same name. Water from this location was first marketed in 1859, but its curative powers had long previously been known. The property had been owned for generations by the Ricker family, whose members seem to have benefited greatly from the waters. Around 1800 Joseph Ricker was brought back from "death's door" through their potency—he lived another fifty-two years; then, in 1827, Wentworth Ricker recovered from a case of the "gravel" after drinking some of the life-

giving fluid. Such a good thing couldn't be kept in the family forever, and when the spring water cured his dyspepsia in 1844, Hiram Ricker decided to go into business. After some years of using unmarked containers, Ricker designed the most famous of all minerals, the Moses bottle, a figural in the form of a bearded man sitting on a rock. The inspiration for this shape supposedly came from the biblical legend of Moses striking his shaft on a rock in the territory of Horeb and causing water to flow forth. The first of the new bottles were manufactured in 1876 by the Salem Glass Works of Salem, New Jersey. Since that time no less than forty variants of the bottle have been produced, not all of them for mineral water.

Unlike many of the famous nineteenth-century spas, Poland Springs has survived and prospered to the present day. The great resort hotel stands, and the waters are bottled for shipment throughout the world.

In Vermont there were several similar resorts. At Sheldon near the Canadian border were the Sheldon and Vermont Springs and the Missisquoi "A" well. Farther south were located the Middletown Healing Springs and the Guilford Spring, in a hamlet just north of the Massachusetts line.

Much less is known of the spas located in western areas of the nation. They do seem to have been numerous, particularly in California and the desert states. The former could boast of Jackson's Napa Soda Springs, the Bartlett Spring, and the Tuscan waters in Tehama County. This last advertised extensively in the 1870s, the following notice being typical:

TUSCAN SPRINGS
Eight miles east of Red Bluff
J. H. Disher, Prop.
The most eminent physicians of San Fran-

cisco and the state, after careful analysis of the waters, pronounce them to be the best mineral springs in the United States. For chronic diseases of all kinds, Rheumatism, Scrofula, Nervous Complaints, etc., . . . no business done on Saturday.

Mineral water bottles tend to be of a standard form, cylindrical, with thick walls, sloping shoulders, and tapered collars. Rare exceptions are the eight-sided blob-top soda forms, two of which are especially interesting. The blue color of these makes them even more uncommon. The one marked "Superior/Mineral Water/Mt. Crawford/Springfield" is particularly fine. While the majority of mineral containers are found in aqua or various shades of green, other colors do occur—blue, amber, red amber, yellow, and teal.

Since most spring water receptacles were manufactured between 1850 and 1890, when the business went into a decline, they were generally formed in a mold and held in a snap case. A tiny percentage of early pieces have open pontils; a few more show the mark of the iron pontil. All employed a cork closure.

The otherwise prosaic surfaces of these vessels are enlivened by a variety of embossed letterings reflecting the many proprietors once active in the business. More interesting, however, are the scarce figurative embossings. Most in demand is the bust of Washington that appears on the Washington Spring bottle from Ballston Spa, New York. There are also containers, such as the Saratoga Geyser and Glaceier Spring bottles from Saratoga, that bear the figure of a spout of water or artesian well head.

As they were produced in such great numbers, mineral water vessels, particularly those from the Saratoga spas, are relatively abundant. At present, however, there is great interest in this field; prices have gone up sharply, and all but the most common brands have become difficult to obtain. Being sturdy bottles, minerals often survive in dumps, and diggers frequently come across them. For those who choose to buy, most bottle dealers and shows will offer a few specimens.

SODA WATER BOTTLES

The saturation of water with carbonic acid gas to produce carbonated water was a technique first developed by Joseph Priestley, the English scientist. Manufacturers who had long recognized that bubbly mineral waters were generally much more popular than the still variety quickly took Priestley's discovery to heart. As early as 1807 an Englishman named Hawkins was granted a patent for an improvement in the original method of production, and it appears that he or one of his partners was selling carbonated water before 1809. In fact, during the first decade of the nineteenth century, installations for the production of carbonated water or the carbonation of natural mineral water were established in Philadelphia, Boston, New Haven, and Charleston, South Carolina.

Artificial carbonated water was not manufactured on a large scale until the 1830s, when John Matthews of New York City began to make and bottle the beverage for extensive distribution. Matthews's business was so large that he was able to acquire and utilize all the scrap marble chips—which were broken down to form carbonic acid—from the building of Saint Patrick's Cathedral, enough raw material for twenty-five million gallons of soda water.

Initially, carbonation had been used primarily to enliven mineral waters, and the attempt, in 1807, of a Philadelphia producer to add fruit juice to carbonated water did

Top: Detail of Congress & Empire Spring E   118
mineral water bottle. *Above:* Green mineral
waters: two Congress & Empire Spring Co.
C bottles, "Congress Water" on reverse;
Congress & Empire Spring Co. E, "Empire Water"
on reverse. (All, courtesy H. and B. Shatoff)

not prove popular. During the late 1830s, however, flavored soda water became the rage, with "soda fountains" opening in many cities and competitors vying in the number of tasty variations they could achieve. Since then, carbonated beverages have become one of the mainstays (though hardly a healthy one) of American culture.

It is uncertain what form of container was preferred for the storage and distribution of early carbonated water. Both demijohns and stoneware jugs or bottles were used for the product, as was the case with mineral waters. In any case, a sturdy vessel was required, and this need was met by development of the "blob-top" soda. This type of soda bottle (two are illustrated) is generally small, often holding less than a half pint. It has a shallow sloping shoulder and a large applied collar—the so-called blob top. In order for the cork to sit firmly under pressure of the contents, a wire was wrapped around and under the collar, then bound across the cork, fixing it securely in place. Blob tops are often extremely thick-walled, and the earliest (ca. 1830) show pontil scars. Iron pontil specimens are somewhat more plentiful, but the great majority have the smooth base associated with use of the snap case.

In the second half of the last century manufacturers began to transport carbonated water in larger containers, quarts and gallons. While some of these had cork closures like the earlier bottles, most used the Hutchinson stopper, which consisted of a rubber gasket fixed between two metal plates and attached to a spring wire stem. A loop on this stem extended above the neck of the bottle while the rest of the rig was below the mouth. After the bottle was filled one grasped the loop and pulled up the rubber disk until it fit firmly against the bottle shoulder held in

Sun-colored amethyst soda water bottle, embossed "Martin & McCarthy, Riverside, N.Y."

place by the pressure of the contents. The Hutchinson closure, invented in 1879, remained popular until replaced by the modern crown cork, which was developed in 1891.

Later sodas had much thinner walls than their predecessors and tended to be made of clear or aqua glass. Blob tops, on the other hand, while most common in aqua, are found in green, amber, and, rarely, blue. A blue example, embossed "Knickerbocker Soda Water," is known.

Also known is a rare sea-green torpedo soda. (The torpedo shape was supposedly intended to prevent the bottle from being stood upright, which could dry out the cork and cause loss of seal.) Perhaps the rarest of all hues in this category is yellow. One of the few specimens known in this shade is the blob-top George Beck's Wine Soda bottle. This is an interesting container, because the embossing indicates that alcoholic spirits were employed to enliven its contents.

Embossing on sodas is primarily of interest in providing information about manufacturers and localities. Many collectors try to develop groups of different bottles relating to a single geographical area. Figurative embossing is less common. There was little of it on the blob tops; one rare example, a raised eagle, is worth noting. Human figures also appear on some early receptacles, but the larger and later soda water containers were most likely to bear detailed scenes—for example, the New York City clear glass quart shown on page 113, which has an interesting representation of a bartender plying his trade.

Interest in sodas is somewhat recent, and the common specimens, particularly those with twentieth-century crown cork closures, are relatively easy to come by. Hutchinsons and blob tops are harder to find, particularly those with open or iron pontils or with unusual embossments. The later bottles are frequently found in dumps or old storage places, since they are sturdy and survive well. Not all bottle dealers handle sodas, but these bottles are coming into their own and appear more and more frequently both at shows and in dealers' advertisements.

Opposite top: Mineral water bottles. From left to right: aqua, Quaker Springs; aqua, Massena Spring Water; green, Haskins Spring Company. *Left:* Aqua Saratoga mineral waters. From left to right: Triton Spouting Spring; Glacier Spouting Spring; Washington Lithia Well; Geyser Spring. (All, courtesy Robert Pattridge)

10
Perfume, Scent, and Cologne Bottles

Above: Figural perfume bottles: milk glass figure, embossed "Billikin, The God of Things As They Ought to Be"; black glass shoe with screw top. (Courtesy Burton Spiller) *Opposite:* Clear flint glass perfume bottle with ground pontil.

Perfume, scent, and cologne containers have a long and interesting history. A wide variety of these small receptacles have been found in the tombs and ruins of Mideastern civilizations, and it is evident that the use of sweet-smelling fluids to mask unpleasant odors and to provide a pleasant atmosphere has been a custom for thousands of years.

Accordingly, it is not surprising to learn that perfume, scent, and cologne bottles were among the earliest made in this country. Henry William Stiegel—probably the first American glass manufacturer to produce mold-blown bottles—is known to have manufactured both perfume and scent containers. Account books for his Manheim, Pennsylvania, glassworks list 584 "smelling bottles" and 6,214 "pocket" (perfume) bottles on hand or disposed of in the period between 1769 and 1770.

Perfume, or "essence," is distinguished from scent both by use and composition. Perfume was and still is used to enhance personal presence, at first by masking body odor, in a day when bathing was infrequent, and today as a matter of taste. Scent, or smelling salts, on the other hand, is perfume plus ammonia, a pungent salt whose acrid vapors are used to revive those who feel faint—a condition that, judging from the quantity of scent containers, was much more common with our grandmothers than with modern women.

Above: Light blue milk glass cologne bottle from
Sandwich Glass Factory. (Courtesy Emil Walter)
Opposite: Embossed aqua rococo-style cologne
bottles blown in a three-piece mold. From left
to right: basket of flowers, ship, and rooster.
(Courtesy Jim Wetzel)

Stiegel's amethyst perfume bottles were about a half pint in size, globular in shape, with a short cylindrical neck and plain lip. Several different molds were employed in the making of these containers, including ribbed and diamond patterns. Stiegel's shop also made attractive scent or smelling salts vessels. These were tiny receptacles, no more than three inches high. They were blown in a ribbed pattern mold, which produced a vertical or right-hand swirl ridging much like a modern Christmas tree light. One of the earliest of these bottles bears a paper label:

Pungent
Smelling Salts
Prepared
And Sold By
GEO. BRINLEY
Druggist

Stiegel smelling salts were made in a spectacular variety of colors—sapphire and cobalt blue, violet, purple, green, yellow, puce, amethyst, opalescent, and clear.

Many other eighteenth- and nineteenth-century glasshouses manufactured containers for smelling salts. They were free-blown, often in elaborate shapes—such as the sea horse bottle whose body was drawn out in the form of a tail, then curled back against itself; or formed in dip molds; or finally, as the nineteenth century progressed, shaped in full-size two-piece molds similar to those used for historical flasks. In this last group one is likely to find concentric ring designs, ribbing, sunbursts, and even the scroll shape so dear to flask collectors. In the waning years of the nineteenth century, scent bottle forms became much less ornate. These rather common mold-blown vessels are primarily of geometric or tubular shape and generally appear in emerald green glass, and less often in cobalt and yellow. A group of such vessels is shown (page 129).

One of the major sources of smelling salts was the Boston and Sandwich Glass Company, which was active from 1825 to 1888. Some of its products were blown and then decorated with cut patterns; but the majority were mold-formed, some in simple geometric shapes, others as figurals, such as the miniature acorn-shaped vessels whose fragments have been excavated on the site of the former factory.

Perfume bottles were also made at the Boston and Sandwich works. Many were of pressed glass in the same basic patterns used for lamp fonts, vases, and other larger objects. They were also produced in cased glass and in simple geometric forms similar to those used for scent bottles. An example of the latter in a particularly rich hue is known; it is only three inches high.

Another major manufacturer of perfumes was the South Boston Flint Glass Works. An advertisement by this firm in the *Columbian Centinel* of January 17, 1816, listed "essence phials" as among the products offered for sale. None of these objects has as yet come to light.

Cologne bottles appeared at a much later date than perfume and smelling salts containers and are, consequently, found in larger quantities today. Cologne is perfume diluted with alcohol so that it is neither as strong nor as lasting in effect as the more concentrated fluid. Since a much larger amount is required to achieve the same effect, cologne bottles are generally larger than perfumes. They first appeared in glass factory inventories around 1830. The New England Glass Bottle Company price list for November 1, 1829, mentions "Lavender Bottles" in a pint

size. These are almost certainly colognes; they sold for $7.50 per gross. It was not until the middle of the century that cologne assumed sufficient popularity for the containers to be seen frequently in company stock.

Perfumes and scents had always appeared in attractive, often figural, bottles; and the same tradition was established for colognes. While there are a few plain, clear glass vessels—such as the unembossed pontiled bottle with Jenny Lind Cologne label that is illustrated—the majority are highly decorative. Classic forms abound—the blue milk glass receptacle shown is particularly graceful— and geometrics are frequently encountered. The tower is rather unusual; while the cathedral bottle, not a common form, is no doubt similar to the "14 Gross Catherial Colognes" that were sold on May 1, 1847, by the Coventry Glass Factory Company of Coventry, Connecticut. Since the purchaser, W. G. Foreman, also took three gross "rose colognes" and an equal number of "2 oz. colognes," it may be assumed that this company produced a rather diversified selection.

Animal and human figurals frequently appear among colognes and are most popular. Many of these were shaped from clear or aqua glass, as well as opalescent, blue, amber, green, and several types of milk glass. A representative sample is shown—a lady with muff, a court jester. The third vessel in the picture is a scroll bottle featuring the embossed face and name of a child, Charlie Ross. This cologne, produced around 1880, commemorates the most famous kidnapping of the nineteenth century. The Ross child was abducted on July 1, 1874, and was never seen again, though his father, a wealthy merchant, spent substantial sums on advertising and rewards. The bottle appears to have been a last, hopeless effort.

126

Aqua pontiled cologne with label reading
"Jenny Lind Cologne" and lithographed
figure. (Courtesy Andrew A. Goldman)

Other figurals, two illustrated here, are a baby, a standing man, a black milk glass shoe, and an unusual milk glass figure embossed "Billiken/the God of/Things As They/Ought to Be." These are but a small sample of the several hundred known figural colognes. The ledgers of the glassmaker Solomon H. Stanger for the years 1848–1852 showed that he made colognes in grape, fancy, tree, fountain, lion, dahlia, and several diamond patterns. And it should be emphasized that Stanger ran a small shop in South Jersey. Larger companies like Sandwich and the numerous Pittsburgh firms had a much more extensive selection of forms.

For the collector of perfume, scent, and cologne containers, bottle dealers must be the primary source; and even here, certain types such as the Stiegels are virtually unattainable, except at those rare times when a long-established collection is broken up. The Sandwich glass geometrics and the later figurals may be located, though often at impressive prices. The very nature of these vessels made them keepsakes or curiosities, and very few found their way to the dump or attic. As a result, they are seldom recovered from these sources. For specific items the best system is to advertise in antiques and bottle publications.

Opposite: Aqua figural colognes. From left to right: lady with muff; bottle with name and portrait of kidnapped child, Charlie Ross; clown. (Courtesy B. Spiller) *Above:* Smelling salts. Reclining container is yellow; others are green. (Courtesy Joan and Larry Kindler)

Opposite: Cone-shaped inks in various colors. (Courtesy George Anderson) *Left:* Master inks. From left to right: Top row: Harrison's Columbian Ink; E. W. Waters, Troy; two unmarked bottles. Bottom row: J. M. Butler's; three blue S. S. Stafford's. *Below:* Teakettle inks in various colors. (Courtesy Joan and Larry Kindler)

some of Maynard and Noyes's customers were well pleased. For example, in 1848 the secretary of Boston's Merchants Insurance Company advised the proprietors that "I have used your writing ink for the last sixteen years. In 1840, I gave you a certificate of its excellence and have continued its use ever since to my entire satisfaction. My opinion is confirmed in its superiority. It flows freely from the pen and is in all respects the best ink I have ever used."

Long-lived ink manufacturers like Maynard and Noyes and the well-known Carter were the exception. Most ink makers appear to have worked for only a few years, so that embossed or labeled bottles bearing their names are often hard to find, a fact that enhances collector interest. Often the only record left will be an advertisement, such as one placed long ago by a hopeful producer: "STEPHENS WRITING FLUID . . . just received a new supply of Stephens Unchangeable Light Blue Writing Fluid put up in large and small bottles, for sale by Spaldings & Sons, 192 Main St." (*Hartford Courant,* May 15, 1840).

Rarity is an attraction in the collection of inks, but not the only one. At least as many enthusiasts are attracted by the great variations in form and color. Since inkwells and the smaller early bottles, which doubled as wells, were generally exposed to view on a desk or table, there was an effort to create attractive forms.

The basic ink bottle shape is a cone tapering up from a wide bottom to a narrow neck. This configuration is both pleasing to the eye and practical; the concentration of weight in the heavy base minimizes tipping, an important consideration in the days of quill pens, since the pen was dipped into the well or bottle many times in the course of a day's work. Conical bottles are either plain or paneled; the latter have six, eight, ten, twelve, or sixteen sides and were generally known as "umbrellas." Early advertisers employed the terms "cone stand" and "fluted cone stand" respectively to distinguish between these styles. No other ink bottle form appears in as great a color variety as the cone. The group of plain cones pictured here ranges in color from clear to black glass and includes exceedingly rare examples in yellow and teal.

Umbrellas are even more attractive. Being for the most part older—many are pontiled—they combine an exciting glass texture with smoky colors enhanced by the attractive geometric form. Many of the umbrella inks were produced in early New England glasshouses, but few bear the embossing of either maker or user.

A near relative of the cone is the domed bottle with a central neck, essentially a semicircular form with the mouth at the midpoint of the curved side. The example shown is unusually large and may have been a supply bottle. In 1865 the J. and I. E. Moore ink company of Warren, Massachusetts, patented a novel version of the domed ink with the neck set off to one side, a characteristic responsible for the name "turtle" ink. As may be seen from the illustration, turtles come in a variety of attractive shades.

The great majority of ink bottles were made in the cylindrical shape common to a wide variety of utility bottles. In the sizes above a quarter pint, which were employed for shipment or storage, they were called Master inks. Since they were used to fill smaller bottles and wells, they frequently had pouring lips. The three blue Staffords Masters shown here are relatively common and very popular with collectors. On the other hand, the olive green bottle embossed "E. Waters/ Troy" is an apparently unique example.

Left: Aqua figural inks. The one at right is embossed "Pat. March 10, 1870." *Below:* Snail inkstands with cast-iron pen racks. At left, aqua; at right, milk glass. (Courtesy Joan and Larry Kindler)

Below: Conical inks. *Right:* A major group of ink bottles. *Bottom:* Aqua inks with pen rests. *Opposite:* Turtle inks. From left to right: Top row: J&M Co.; J&M Co.; JHEM Co. Middle row: all marked "J&IEM Co." Bottom row: unmarked. (All, courtesy Joan and Larry Kindler)

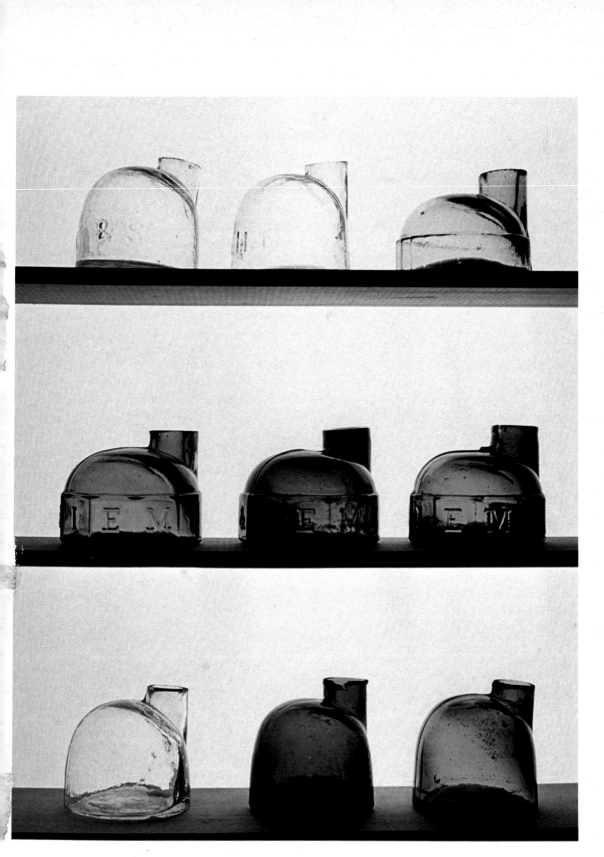

Square and rectangular inks are also common. The former were seldom made before 1860, and pontiled examples are uncommon. In the late nineteenth and early twentieth centuries the form proliferated, the slope shoulder variation being the most often seen. Due to some vague resemblance to a square building with central chimney, this was termed a "schoolhouse" ink.

Rectangular specimens often have one or two shallow pen ledges running horizontally across the upper body surface. These slots, which were intended as a place where the quill or steel pen might rest when not in use, emphasize the fact that many ink bottles served also as inkwells. Colors other than aqua are rare in this category.

In inks as in other bottles the most sought-after containers are the figurals. Barrels, ships, shoes, houses, hats, and a host of other decorative receptacles have held writing fluid. The oldest perhaps are the barrels. Beginning with its use as a campaign symbol by William Henry Harrison in 1840, the barrel-shaped ink bottle appeared in various sizes and patterns up to the end of the nineteenth century. A pontiled barrel like those illustrated, embossed with the name of Wm. E. Bonney, an ink manufacturer of South Hanover, Massachusetts, is one of the earliest known. It was also during Harrison's campaign for the presidency that the first house- or log-cabin-shaped inks appeared. A few pontil-marked examples are known, but most date from a later period, as, for example, an extremely fine flint glass house.

The locomotive-shaped container patented by Charles L. Lochman in 1874 is among the most prized of figurals. So pleased was the proprietor with this unique form that he advertised his writing fluid as "Lochman's Locomotive Ink." Much more common are banana-shaped receptacles, such as the one illustrated here. The configuration in this case, while unusual, was clearly intended to be practical—to prevent spillage—rather than decorative.

Inkwells have been manufactured of many materials—pottery, metal, stone, rubber, and wood, among others. Those made of glass, however, are among the most attractive. The early free-blown specimens are rare and difficult to authenticate. They vary in form from simple basins to extremely ornate loop-decorated pieces in the South Jersey tradition. Foreign pieces both old and new may be confused with this type, and collectors are advised to proceed with caution.

Much more is known of the so-called Pitkin-type well, which was made by expanding a gather of glass in a ribbed part mold. The pattern thus obtained was then withdrawn and reshaped by twisting the hot metal right or left, after which the newly swirled gather was blown into a full-size inkwell mold. This well style was produced by glass factories in Connecticut, New Hampshire, Pennsylvania, and Ohio.

During the period 1815–1840, three-piece full-size molds were used to manufacture a wide assortment of inkwells in various attractive geometric patterns. During the first half of the nineteenth century the production of blown three-mold objects—they include nearly every type of tableware in addition to wells—approached mass production in volume. Nevertheless, ink containers of this type are not common. Since nearly all production had ceased by 1850, the great majority of such wells are pontil-marked. They are also found primarily in some variation of "black glass"—that is, dark green, olive, or amber. Like most early inkwells and unlike ink bottles, these receptacles are seldom marked with a manufacturer's name.

Shown is an interesting group of fountain-type wells, popularly known as "tea-kettles" because of the neck or spout extending up at an angle from the base. Teakettles have been found in a dozen colors, among which the amethyst shade shown here must be considered choice. While one style bears the embossed notice of application for a United States patent, most teakettles are unmarked and may be confused with similar European inkwells.

Somewhat related to the above are the so-called igloo-type fountains. In these inks the main well is dome-shaped, bearing some resemblance to an Eskimo igloo. Igloos appear in many variations and are rarely encountered in anything other than clear glass. They are also, for the most part, relatively late. Few bear a true pontil mark.

The two revolving inkwells illustrated are of a type known to collectors as "snails." They consist of a glass fountain, which is indeed snail-shaped, mounted on a cast-iron frame. Patent dates appearing on the frames indicate that revolving inkwells were popular chiefly in the 1870s and 1880s. They come in a very limited range of color—clear, cobalt, and milk glass.

There is also a wide variety of simple round or square wells of the sort still made today. Some of them were formed from clear flint or cut glass; others were decorated by etching or the use of enamel paint. Blue, green, and red glass bodies were other popular types.

True figurals are less common among wells than among ink bottles. A boot is known and a most spectacular pressed glass ink stand in the form of Philadelphia's Memorial Hall. This piece, embossed "Memorial Hall/Patent Appld for/Charles Yockel Estab. 1855/235 Bread St. Philada Pa. USA Glass Mold Maker," was intended to serve as a remembrance of the Philadelphia Centennial of 1876.

There is substantial collector interest in ink bottles and inkwells, and those seeking them will find prices high, particularly for examples in color. The earlier types were primarily produced in New England, Pennsylvania, and Ohio, and previously unidentified examples are likely to come from those areas, chiefly as the result of excavation. The numerous registered patents for which there are no known representations hold out the exciting possibility of new discoveries. For those who prefer to avoid shovel work, most bottle shows and the frequent bottle auctions in all areas of the country will present an opportunity to obtain interesting additions to a collection.

Figural ink in shape of a banana, embossed "Pat'd 1876." (Courtesy Joan and Larry Kindler)

12
FOOD BOTTLES

Above: Embossed aqua cathedral pickle jars in Gothic design, one in quart size, two in gallon size. (Courtesy Burton Spiller) *Opposite:* Aqua food jars. From left to right: spiral embossed pepper sauce; Gothic pickle; Gothic pepper sauce. (Courtesy Jim Wetzel)

Food preservation has been a major concern of mankind since before the dawn of recorded history. Many centuries ago it was discovered that spoilage might be curtailed either by drying or by pickling. Drying involved removing the moisture content of the foodstuffs, which prevented deterioration. Pickling involved immersing the food in a preservative such as salt, sugar, alcohol, or vinegar.

Only a limited number of foods could be preserved in these ways, and then at a substantial loss of flavor and color. Moreover, of the foods thus cured, a large number could not be stored in bottles. Accordingly, before the development of modern canning methods in the mid-nineteenth century (see the next chapter), the variety of what might be called food containers was rather limited. Among the substances preserved by drying, chocolate was perhaps most common. An early Dutch chocolate bottle is illustrated in a later chapter; also known is a twentieth-century version of such a container. Made by the Wan-Eta Cocoa Company of Boston, Massachusetts, it was intended to be used as a preserve jar when its original contents were exhausted.

Since in order to be eaten chocolate must be mixed with milk or other liquid, it may be thought of as an early form of the dehydrated food so popular with modern outdoorsmen. However, there were other lesser-known but similar substances as well. On

140

Above: Extremely large vasiform embossed
pickle jars with floral decoration. Center
jar is two feet tall. (Courtesy Jim Wetzel)
Opposite: Aqua striated pepper sauce bottle.

generally found in some shade of aqua or green; other colors such as cobalt and milk glass are rare exceptions. Earlier examples are frequently pontil-marked.

Cooking and medicinal oils were sold in long-necked cylindrical bottles, which were rarely embossed in any way. These were, apparently, a common form. A note on a bill of lading from the New England Glass Works to a New York City customer in 1832 mentioned that "we have only 9 gross Long Castor Oils on hand—these we send and next week will forward the remainder of the 15 gross mentioned in yrs. of the 23rd. inst."

Again, in 1827 the same company listed twenty dozen oil bottles among the wares offered for sale through the *Boston Commercial Gazette*.

It should also be noted that oil bottles or similar containers were used for vinegar. Since usually neither type was embossed, only the presence of an identifying manufacturer's label allows us to distinguish between the two. Oils and vinegars were usually made of plain aqua bottle glass, though oils in blue have been identified.

Syrup, due to its high sugar content, can also withstand rot. Moreover, due to the relative blandness of the pioneer diet, sweets for cooking or other consumption were a popular item. An advertisement in the *Boston Daily Advertiser* for June 14, 1834, noted that the New England Glass Bottle Company had no less than "300 Gross Green Syrup Bottles" for sale. At a later date, samples of a popular maple syrup were distributed in the lovely miniature ear-of-corn bottles shown here. Flavoring syrups were particularly popular in the last century, since fresh fruit was available only for a few months each year. In November, 1867, the Santa Cruz, California, *Times* advertised one of these compounds: "Redington's Flavoring Extract . . . made from fresh fruits. Each bottle holds twice as much as any other brand on the market, consequently, it is the cheapest and the best."

Similar to the flavorings were the concentrated syrups from which early soft drinks were made. Hires, Coca Cola, and less successful competitors sold concentrates from which a drink could be produced by the addition of carbonated water.

Sugar was, of course, a common preservative, being particularly employed in the safeguarding of fruits and berries. On page 7 is a tall ten-sided container colloquially referred to in New England as a "Huckelberry Bottle" and believed to have been used for the storage of blueberries or similar pulpy fruit. These receptacles were sealed with a cork and wax and have been found with the original contents intact. It is known that such bottles were manufactured at the Westford, Connecticut, Glass Company between 1857 and 1873 as well as at the nearby Willington works.

The advent of the airtight screw top and, later, the automatic bottle-making machine led to the proliferation of food bottles. There are thousands of late nineteenth- and early

twentieth-century variations, and collectors so far have shown no great interest in any other than the figurals. A great many of the bottles dug from dumps will fall into the area of food containers; it is the one area where collecting remains inexpensive. Earlier types, such as pickle and pepper sauce bottles, are in greater demand and are available only at substantial cost.

147

13
FRUIT JARS

Above: Rare aqua fruit jar, embossed "Imperial,"
ground glass lip and three-prong cover clamp.
Opposite: Aqua fruit jars with clamp hinge
closures. From left to right: Gregory's
Patent; Favorite; The Winslow Improved Valve
Jar. (All, courtesy Richard Van Der Laan)

One form of food container, the fruit jar, is
the focus of such extensive collector interest
as to justify separate treatment. Moreover,
the development of this receptacle is typical
of American response to a recognized problem. Early food bottles were not airtight and
would not prevent decay; they were, rather,
designed to maintain the moisture of the contents and to prevent dust from entering food
substances that through drying or pickling
were already more or less impervious to rot.

The fruit or canning jar was intended to
provide an airtight storage container for
food sterilized by boiling, which could be
maintained in a sterile state—and thereby
kept from rotting—only by preventing its con-
tamination by airborne bacteria.

The discoverer of canning as a way of
food preservation was the Frenchman Nicolas
Appert, who in 1810 published *The Art of
Preserving*. This work was the outcome of
fifteen years' research spurred on by a large
reward offered by the Napoleonic government. Appert's theory was a simple one: en-
close the food in a glass container, seal it airtight, then boil the container until all micro-
organisms are dead. Such a system would
maintain natural taste and color while eliminating the need for salting, pickling, or drying. Needless to say, it had an immediate
appeal. Appert's book was published in this
country in 1812, and the first canning jars appeared soon after. They were free-blown

cylindrical vessels with wide mouths and a flaring collar. Three fine examples from Pennsylvania are illustrated here. Preserve jars, as they were then called, appear frequently in the inventories and advertisements of early nineteenth-century glasshouses. The New England Glass Bottle Company was making them in 1829 in three sizes—pint, quart, and two quart. Similar types are known to have been manufactured at Stoddard, New Hampshire, in the 1840s and 1850s.

The flanged-mouth preserve jar was sealed by pouring hot wax on top of the contents until the mass was even with the bottle top. Then a piece of oiled or waxed linen cloth was tied over the jar top to prevent the seal from being broken. However, a wax seal could not take much rough handling or even tipping; and so the system proved generally inefficient. A better technique involved the use of bottles with a vertical neck and much narrower mouth. Into these, a thick cork or section of corncob was driven to provide a hermetical seal. To achieve a tight fit the cork was often wrapped in cloth or paper, then covered with wax or a tin top, which fit down over the neck of the bottle. An example of a jar with this type of closure is the Newman's Patent jar.

By the mid-nineteenth century an improved form of wax-seal jar had been developed. It had an inside ledge or ridge running about the neck, onto which a circle of heavy waxed paper or a matching glass or tin disk might be fitted. An expanded portion of the bottle neck above this area was then filled with a layer of hot paraffin. Though not the final answer, the seal achieved was firm and with care could last for a long time. Three of these "wax sealers," all in the extremely rare cobalt blue, are known.

Though they continued to be manufac-

tured throughout the last century, wax-seal bottles gradually were replaced by screw-top fruit jars. The first of these was developed by John Landis Mason, a New York City tinsmith. In 1858 he patented a mold that would produce a glass fruit jar with a threaded neck; an example of the original design as illustrated here. For his threaded jar, Mason designed a matching zinc lid; and in March of 1869 Lewis R. Boyd completed the picture

by patenting an opal glass liner for the lid, thus preventing harmful contact between the metal and the preserved food. The complete unit proved to be both cheap and effective. The use of a standard mold assured that bottle mouths would be uniform and could receive the matching caps. Unlike earlier pewter screw tops, the zinc fittings were sturdy and could take the pressure necessary to form a hermetical seal. The inventor, in time, licensed both his patents to mass manufacturers, and within a few years, the Mason jar was synonymous with food preservation. Mason, on the other hand, shared the fate of so many other innovators—he died poor and unheralded.

During the legal life of Mason's patent, would-be competitors were faced with the problem of producing a similar but noninfringing closure. As a result, a remarkable

Canton Electric Fruit Jar and amber Globe, similar to jars illustrated here. Bail-type closures continue, even today, to compete for the housewives' favor with the earlier screw-type top.

The various forms of closure and the array of unusual decorative embossings are the chief attractions of canning jars. The embossings are particularly interesting, consisting of human and animal figures and a wide variety of objects. The head of Lafayette, an unusual item, is a most sought-after example, and the Flaccus Brothers cow is also much in demand. Glass and fruit jar makers also often placed their initials on the bottles in ornate scrollwork, and these ciphers greatly enhance otherwise uninteresting jars.

The receptacles themselves are for the most part monotonously alike. The glass-making firm of Potter and Bodine of Bridgeton, New Jersey, manufactured a barrel-shaped wax sealer in the late 1850s. Four-, eight-, and twelve-sided and ovoid jars are also known. The vast majority, however, are plain cylinders with short necks.

Color also is greatly limited. Various shades of aqua and clear glass predominate, with a limited number of amber jars. Milk glass, emerald green, and black are much harder to come by, with examples in blue extremely scarce; when they are available, they may command over a thousand dollars each.

In general, however, fruit jars are readily available to the collector. Ball, Mason Lightning, and other major brands are found in vast numbers throughout the country. While most of them are machine-made, large numbers of hand-finished, ground-top bottles may be obtained for a modest investment. Wax sealers are less common, and rare colors or closures usually appear only at bottle shows or in private collections.

variety of clamps, screws, and other devices were developed. The most effective of them, and the prototype for modern clamp-seal jars, was patented in 1875 by Charles de Quillfeldt and put into production by the glassmaker Henry Putnam. It entailed the use of an all-glass top and a rubber ring, which were securely locked to the bottle mouth by an iron bail seated on the jar neck. Similar closures may be seen on the blue

Rare pontiled barrel-shaped aqua fruit jars. From left to right: Ravenna Glass Works; two jars marked "Potter & Bodine Airtight Fruit Jar." (Courtesy Richard Van Der Laan)

14
MILK BOTTLES

Above: One-pint milk bottles in clear glass. At left, embossed "Absolutely Pure Milk, The Milk Protector"; at right, embossed "B. C. Patterson Milk & Cream, Golden Farm." (Courtesy Jim Wetzel) *Opposite:* Clear glass milk bottle patented 1898, with tin handle and bail-type closure. (Courtesy Burton Spiller)

The transportation and preservation of fresh milk presented a major problem for suppliers until nearly the end of the nineteenth century. For generations, milk was delivered to market in cans or earthen crocks and doled out to the consumer, who carried it home in his own pail or bottle. Increasing concern with sanitation as well as an expanding urban market encouraged development of a more efficient method of distribution. Central to this problem was an adequate container. It is said that one Alexander Campbell was delivering milk to Brooklyn customers in bottles as early as 1878, but the milk bottle patent issued March 23, 1880, to the Warren Glass Works Company is the first known in this field. The Warren bottle was in production in 1881 and was distributed in New York City by A. V. Whiteman of 72 Murray Street. Three years later the so-called Whiteman Milk Jar was patented, and the same year Dr. Henry D. Thatcher, a Potsdam, New York, druggist, invented a milk bottle with a closure similar to that employed on the Lightning fruit jar—that is, a bail-type fastener. The Thatcher container was the first embossed milk bottle. The quaint raised design of a farmer milking a cow was the forerunner for a wide variety of decorated receptacles. Flags, stars, birds, buildings, animals, and human figures have all served to grace these humble vessels.

Thatcher was not content with a single

Embossed clear glass milk bottles. From left to right: F. E. Reed, Maple Grove Dairy; Thatcher Mfg. Co.; People's Dairy Co. (Courtesy J. Brown)

triumph. In 1886 he developed a glass closure for his bottle, and three years later he revolutionized the industry by introducing the Common Sense Milk Jar, which had a groove inside the bottle upon which rested a heavily waxed paper cap. In the next twenty years the great majority of milk bottle makers began to use wide-mouth bottles and this cheap and sanitary closure. As Thatcher himself noted in his advertising materials, there were "no rusty metal covers or twisted wire fasteners, less breakage and [the bottle] can be washed absolutely clean and much quicker than any other . . . avoiding tainted or sour milk."

The vast majority of milk bottles date

from the era of the automatic bottle machine; it is difficult to obtain pre-1900 specimens, particularly the narrow-mouthed form with the Lightning closure. A most interesting example from the early period is shown here. It bears an 1898 patent date and an unusual iron-bound handle, which, while it would have facilitated handling, did not catch on, probably because it prevented packing the bottles in a milk crate.

Embossed decoration is the major attraction of milk bottles, since there are only a few basic forms—round, square, squat, and cream top (a container with a bulbous upper section in which cream could collect). Most producers marked their bottles, and many added houses, barns, animals—particularly cows—human figures, or patriotic symbols.

The colors of milk bottles is also limited. Most consumers insisted on a clear glass vessel so that they could easily see the milk, and it is difficult to find bottles in any other shade. It is true that quite a few amber containers were made, since many manufacturers felt that this shade retarded souring. Nevertheless, the amber bottles are but a tiny portion of the total milk bottle production. Only one other color appears to have been used— green. The bottle marked "Altacrest Farms/ Spencer, Mass." and bearing the embossed head of a cow has been known for some time, and many believe it to be the only green milk bottle, though there actually are others. One example is the lovely emerald bottle bearing the embossed mark "Brighton Place Dairy/ Rochester, N. Y." While this piece may be unique, it is most likely that other green bottles will come to light.

Milk containers range in size from inch-high samples to gallon bottles, and the collector has many to choose from. In fact, most who follow this branch of the hobby collect only the containers from their own area. Though today substantially replaced by paper or plastic receptacles, milk bottles can still be found in great numbers, so great in fact that with the exception of rare specimens few are offered by antique or bottle dealers. This is one of the few areas of bottle collecting where junk shops, attics, and dumps are still the primary source.

15
HOUSEHOLD BOTTLES

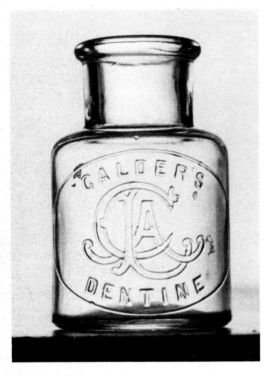

Above: Clear glass tooth-powder container, embossed "Calder's Dentine." *Opposite:* Rare set, four baby feeding bottles embossed "Woodbury Sterilizer," with pewter tops and iron storage frame. (Courtesy S.I. Historical Society)

There are a large number of bottles, some quite unusual in shape or color, which do not fall readily into any presently recognized category of bottle collecting. Among them are containers for skin, hair, and facial aids, tooth powders, household dyes, glues, baby bottles, and similar items. Some of them are now attracting collector interest, but others present the possibility of new and inexpensive areas for exploration.

Perhaps the largest categories and the most interesting are those concerned with personal beauty. The vast number of skin lotions, blemish removers, hair dyes, and hair restorers appearing on the market during the last half of the nineteenth century make it clear that our ancestors differed little from ourselves in their concern with appearance.

For the Victorian woman, an alabaster skin and long silky hair were minimum social requirements. Since neither of these conditions always occurred naturally, an army of manufacturers hastened to assist in their development. The claims then made by skin aids producers sound strangely familiar to us today. For example, La Rue's Alabaster Cream was proclaimed by its maker to be "the favorite toilet companion, the radiant complexion of the young . . . a remedy for and beautifier of the skin, clearing away freckles, sallowness and other unpleasant effects of age, weather or disease" (*Hartford Courant,* February 15, 1873).

158

The manufacturers of these skin aids used a primitive form of psychological advertising: they often packaged their products in milk glass bottles, using the appearance of the container to represent the effect the user hoped to achieve with the substance itself. Milk glass vessels have long had a special attraction for collectors, and bottles of this type are eagerly sought. Worth noting are two of the most popular—Hagan's Magnolia Balm and Professor I. Hubert's Malvina Lotion. Hagan's claimed it would remove "sallowness, tan, blotches, redness, roughness, pimples and sunburn" and restore a lilylike purity and rounded shape to the neck, arms, and face.

While many of these compounds were claimed to be capable of both whitening the skin and removing the hated freckles, some were listed as specialized aids. Thus, one could obtain bleaches such as Blanche Creme, Bradley's Face Bleach, Palmer's Skin Whitener, or Ruppert's Face Bleach and removers like Anti-Freckle Lotion, Hill's Freckle Lotion, and Kingsbury's Freckle Cream. Both groups often used milk glass bottles as well as cobalt, which appears to have also been much favored.

Other promoters, perhaps more realistic in their claims, represented their products as coverups, nothing more. When a woman applied the white, creamy substance to her face, it would create a pallid appearance until washed or worn off. One such makeup was Laird's Bloom of Youth, which was manufactured by George W. Laird of New York City. Laird's was a particularly popular mixture, sold throughout the country—so popular, in fact, that each bottle bore warning of counterfeits. The label carefully advised users to "see that the name G. W. LAIRD is stamped in the glass on the back of the bottle. None other is genuine."

Not all women could afford or obtain these cosmetics, real or bogus, but all were subject to the same social compulsion to exhibit a clear, pale skin. Accordingly, rural lasses wore bonnets to avoid suntan and devised home remedies to achieve a more desirable complexion. Lemon juice and mud packs, even potentially dangerous mixtures of fresh cream and carbolic acid, were employed to this end, and it is unlikely that they were any less successful than the commercial remedies.

The producers of skin aids were effective promoters. They advertised widely, offered attractive premiums or gifts, and enlisted the assistance of contemporary "glamour girls" and women of prominence. In 1888, the actress Fanny Davenport endorsed Wisdom's Robertine as a "very fine and excellent application for whitening and beautifying the face and hands," and it is said that the singer Adelina Patti ordered Champlin's Liquid Pearl shipped to her in five dozen lots while she was performing in Europe.

But a pale skin was not enough. The hair too must meet current standards, and in this area also, the producers stood ready to offer assistance. A wide variety of invigorators, restorers, and dyes was available to both women and men. Best known of all, perhaps, is Seven Sutherland Sisters Hair Grower. This famous compound was packaged in a rather ordinary-looking clear glass bottle, out of which poured a fortune for seven farm girls from western New York. Analysts reported that Hair Grower contained little but water, alcohol, and coloring matter, but it was astutely promoted, first by Fletcher Sutherland, the father and inventor, then by his ambitious daughters. They all had hair several feet in length and regularly went out on tour to show the faithful that their

Early black glass pontiled baby bottle.
(Courtesy Burton Spiller)

Glue bottles. At left, clear glass John's &
Crosley's American Cement Glue; at right,
aqua pontiled Spalding's Glue.

product really worked. And work it did, for them. The hairy siblings, buoyed by their slogan "It's the Hair, Not the Hat, That Makes a Woman Attractive," sold nearly three million dollars' worth of Hair Grower in the thirty-eight years their product was on the market; they built themselves a magnificent mansion near Lockport, New York, where they entertained in grand fashion and exhibited their collective eccentricities, which included trained dogs, bicycle riding, and rapscallion husbands.

While Hair Grower bottles are more interesting for their history than for their appearance, other vessels in this line are quite attractive. Four such, all in unusual hues, are shown here. The emerald green Hall's Hair Renewer once contained a substance that, it was claimed, "brings the Hair back; no more faded or gray hair. Makes growth more rapid; short hair becomes long hair. Completely removes dandruff; baldness is prevented. Feeds the hair bulbs; new hair grows on bald heads." Though it is doubtful that Hall's could do all this, the present-day value of an emerald green bottle from this maker would go a long way toward paying for a series of the best scalp treatments!

Another rare and valuable specimen is the peacock blue Ayer's Hair Vigor bottle. Dr. J. C. Ayer of Lowell, Massachusetts, produced this particular mixture, which promised to return gray hair to its natural state and vitality. What it really did for the user is hard to determine. What it did for Dr. Ayer is clear. He became a millionaire, the owner of paper and cotton mills, and the founder of Ayer, Massachusetts. Two other scalp invigorators in unusual hues are also shown here. One is a cherry-colored Dr. Tebbett's Physiological Hair Regenerator, the other a violet Mrs. A. Allen's World's Hair Restorer.

The above are examples of an extremely limited group of colored hair aids. Figurals are even less likely to be encountered in this category. At present, I know of only one such vessel. This is the amber Hart's Hair Restorer, which appropriately enough is made in the shape of a heart and is embossed "John Hart & Co."

The vast majority of hair restorers and invigorators were sold in ordinary square or rectangular bottles made of clear or aqua glass. A large number of such compounds were marketed; some of the better known are Wyeth's Sage and Sulphur Hair Remedy, Tebbett's Hair Regenerator, Phoenix Seminola Hair Restorer, and Barry's Tricopherous, the last said to have been first marketed in 1801 and still being sold today.

For men, particularly, hair dyes were also a popular item. Some of these, such as the attractive Ballard's Hair Dye are early enough to bear pontil marks. The majority, however, date to the 1860s or later. An interesting specimen is Hill's Instantaneous Hair and Whisker Dye. As may be seen from the illustration, the use of Hill's involved two steps: application of a fixative found in bottle No. 2 guaranteed relative permanence to the dye contained in bottle No. 1. Most other hair colors were single-step operations. A few of the better known are B. Paul's Henna, Instantaneous Hair Colorine, La Creole Hair Color Restorer, Farr's Gray Hair Restorer, Allen's Vita Hair Color Restorer, and Potter's Walnut Tint Hair Stain. The containers in which these were sold are ordinary clear or aqua glass and seldom of great interest in form. The embossing is often quite fine, however; and the bottles can form the easily obtainable basis for an inexpensive specialized collection.

Somewhat less-often discovered are hair oil and dressing bottles. C. F. Miller Com-

Collectors seeking nursing bottles will have little trouble locating later examples. Those made in the last eighty years or so were often discarded on dumps or in storage places, from which they are emerging as interest increases. Figurals and unusual embossings are at a premium and naturally cost more. It is possible, however, to build a fair collection without great expense, unless one insists on including the early free-blown American and European specimens. These are quite expensive and may generally be obtained only through dealers or advertisements in antiques and bottle publications.

In fact, as previously mentioned, household bottles in general offer the fledgling collector an opportunity to amass an extensive and exciting group without the expenditure of vast sums of money. Facial aids, hair restorers, hair dyes, tooth powders, household glues and dyes, like baby bottles, were produced in vast numbers and remain relatively unfashionable among bottle enthusiasts. All types are frequently encountered by diggers or those who explore old storage places. Moreover, since most containers in most of these categories are of relatively recent vintage, they occur in greater numbers and command lower prices, thus presenting an ideal field for the collector with limited funds.

167

16
Snuff and Blacking Bottles

Above: Shoe blacking bottles, unmarked mold-formed examples. (Courtesy W. J. Geisz) *Opposite:* Early pontiled blacking bottle embossed "A. A. Cooley, Hartford." (Courtesy H. and B. Shatoff)

While somewhat limited in form and color variety, snuff and blacking bottles have been of interest to collectors for many years. Also, since the types are old and continue to be produced today in modified shapes, a substantial number of each are available.

Snuff is essentially powdered tobacco, often scented with various aromatic substances. It may be chewed or, as is generally the case, inhaled through the nose. While snuff boxes in which the devotee carries his daily supply come in a variety of materials, including metal, ceramic, and stone, the commercial container for sale or transfer of the substance is generally made of glass or, in larger sizes, of clay.

Tobacco was discovered on this continent during the course of Columbus's second voyage, and it immediately became popular throughout Europe. The inhaling or "taking" of snuff was initially more popular than smoking; Pierre Lorillard, the first manufacturer in this country, was producing it by 1760. Only nine years later Richard Wistar's notice in the *Pennsylvania Chronicle and Universal Advertiser* listed snuff bottles among the products of his glass factory. Company records indicate that similar containers were being made in the 1780s at the Albany Glass Works near Albany, New York.

The earliest of these bottles are free-blown and may have three to eight sides,

often with beveled corners. Cylindrical and ovoid specimens are also known, though they are harder to obtain. It appears that the use of full-size molds came late to this field, and before the 1870s only a few companies employed snuff bottles marked with their names. Two of these are illustrated, both dating from the perid 1840–1850. The container embossed "E. Roome/Troy, N.Y." is fairly common, but that bearing the raised lettering "JJ Mares/61 Front/N-York" may be unique. The third receptacle in the picture is a very lovely and very ancient Dutch chocolate container, which contained tobacco shreds when found and had, no doubt, been pressed into this service when its original contents were exhausted.

As may be observed in the illustrations, snuff bottles are usually composed of common bottle glass in colors ranging from amber through olive green to yellow. The earlier examples have a particularly attractive texture, with many bubbles and an extremely thin wall. Later bottles are primarily amber and mold-blown or machine-made. Snuff bottles are seldom more than four inches high and differ from the great majority of glass bottles in having little or no neck. There is usually just a sloping shoulder and hand-formed lip into which a flat, wax-covered

cork was set to keep the contents fresh and moist.

Apparently, at one time snuff was believed to have medicinal properties. A Dr. Marshall's Catarrh Snuff is known; and on January 14, 1823, the *Connecticut Courant* carried an advertisement for Aromatic and Headache Snuff which maintained that the substance "is considered a sovereign remedy for recent catarrh and slow nervous headache. It is most fragrant and grateful to the smell and sensibly stimulates the spirits. It is useful in hypochondria, removes drowsiness, and is a complete antidote against contagion." The advertisement further noted that the mixture consisted "primarily of herbs" and was prepared by Dr. John P. Whitwell of Boston, Massachusetts.

Since so few of the earlier manufacturers used embossed bottles, it is difficult to determine how many snuff factories there were. Advertisements are not common and when found seldom correspond to the receptacles used by identified firms. Quite a few labeled snuffs have survived, however, particularly those of Lorillard and his successor, the George W. Helme Company. During the 1870s and 1880s, Helme used several glass snuff containers marked "Helme's Railroad Mills" or "Geo. W. Helme, Co., N.Y." One

Above: Aqua snuff bottle labeled "Dr. Marshall's Aromatic Catarrh & Headache Snuff." (Courtesy Staten Island Historical Society) *Opposite:* Black glass snuff bottle labeled "Ralph's Scotch & Rappee Snuff, Manufactured and Sold by Stewart, Ralph & Co." (Courtesy Joan and Larry Kindler)

of these, interestingly enough, was an amber fruit-jar type put out by the Cohansey Glass Works of Philadelphia.

Shoe-blacking bottles are even more uniform in size, shape, and color than snuffs. Almost all of them are mold-blown, square, and four to six inches high. Typically, they have long straight sides and a short neck. Colors found range from aqua through green black glass and into various shades of amber. The examples shown are typical.

Though one might not expect it in a land of pioneers, Americans showed an early and substantial interest in shoe stains. As early as 1803, the *New York Daily Advertiser* carried one manufacturer's bid for public patronage: "Chymical Blacking in Liquid. N. Smith Chymical Perfumes . . . begs leave to recommend his . . . Chymical Liquid Blacking in jars for shoes, boots and or any kind of leather requiring a beautiful black jet shining gloss . . . 2S., 3d, per jar . . . Factory of N. Smith, No. 6 Liberty Street, N. York."

Embossed blacking containers are, like snuffs, hard to come by. An early example by A. A. Cooley of Hartford, Connecticut, is shown here; another known is the Keene, New Hampshire, specimen by Hutchins and Mason illustrated in McKearin's *American Glass.* Large numbers of blacking bottles were made. The New England Glass Bottle Company advertised them throughout its existence from 1826 to 1845, and they were a standard item at most glasshouses. It appears, however, that labels were employed to identify most blacking makers, and when these wore or washed off, what was left was an attractive but often unidentifiable piece of glass.

Both snuff and blacking bottles have been collected for years, and better examples are not inexpensive. Since they were pro-

duced in large quantities, and since the blacking container, particularly, because of its thick, molded sides was quite durable, dumps, attics, and other out-of-the-way places are still yielding fair quantities of them. To these may be added the offerings of bottle shows and shops. Not many appear at major antiques shows, and they are also uncommon at general auctions, though encountered at auctions specializing in bottles and glass.

Below: Early free-blown snuff bottles. *Right:* Blown two-mold blacking bottles. *Bottom right:* Snuff bottles. From left to right: "JJ Mares 61 Front New York"; food and snuff container, "EGH Dekker Amsterdam"; early pontiled snuff, "E. Roome, Troy." (All, courtesy William J. Geisz)

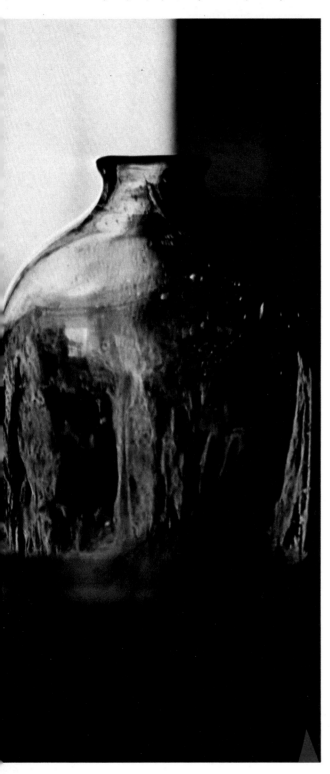

17
DRUG BOTTLES

Until well into the nineteenth century, druggists—or chemists, as they were frequently known—functioned very much like the family doctor, just as they still do in less developed areas of the world. Individuals suffering from any number of maladies could go to them with the assurance that they would prescribe a cure, either one of the readymade proprietary medicines lining their shelves or a concoction they would mix on the spot. For these products the druggists used a variety of bottles, including elaborate receptacles intended more for show than for sale. All of these containers are now considered highly collectible.

Then, as now, the apothecary or druggist was primarily a businessman, secondarily a healer. He advertised regularly and extravagantly, as the following notice will indicate:

Above: Aqua bulk pill bottles, all embossed "Robert Gibson Tablets Manchester England, Made by E. C. Rich, New York." (Courtesy Joan and Larry Kindler) *Opposite:* Early green glass pontiled drug bottle embossed "Henshaw Ward & Co. Druggists Boston." (Courtesy Burton Spiller)

APOTHECARIES HALL, SONORA

The subscriber having just opened a large and commodious drug store in the town of Sonora would respectfully solicit the patronage of physicians and miners. Medicines at wholesale or retail to suit purchasers. All orders promptly attended to; also, a lot of Superior lemon syrup always on hand and for sale on reasonable terms.

(Sonora, California, *Herald,* August 24, 1850)

JOHN E. STROTHERS

He also generally employed a set of two

elaborate and expensive "show bottles" as a sort of trade sign, a device to attract attention. These were massive clear glass vessels, often several feet tall. Some were of a single piece, as in the case of the "silvered glass druggist's show bottle" exhibited at New York City's Crystal Palace in 1853 by the New England Glass Company. Others consisted of three separate vessels that fit one into the other to form a single entity. In either case, the receptacles were filled with colored water—traditionally red, green, and blue—and were placed in a shop window where they provided an attractive and universally recognized symbol of the owner's profession.

That the role of these bottles was something more than mere storage is evidenced from the fact that they were for many years universally known as "Apothecaries' Shop Furniture." In 1816, the Boston Glass Manufactory advertisement in the *Columbian Centinel* for January 17 listed two types of such "furniture," specie mouth show bottles from two gallons to four ounces and salt mouth show bottles in the same range of sizes. Similar containers were offered during the 1820s by the Pittsburgh Glass Works and by Thomas Dyott's factory at Philadelphia. The latter's notice in the *United States Gazette* for March 2, 1825, offered no less than 5,000 gross "Druggists and Confectioners Show Bottles."

It appears, however, that even with this substantial output, many drug bottles were imported, a matter of no small concern to those who were concerned with the well-being of native industries. Thus, the Norwich, Connecticut, *Courier* of July 31, 1816, had occasion to note, in reference to the products of the Boston Glass Manufactory, that "in addition to the Window Glass, there is now made at this manufactory all kinds of glass Chymi-

cal Apparatus and Apothecaries furniture, articles in a high degree useful and necessary, manufactured in a most superior manner, & at such moderate prices as entirely to do away with the necessity of its further importation." Despite the Norwich correspondent's hopes, European bottles, particularly the larger and more ornate examples, have continued to enter this country. As a result, the collector of show bottles must take care to see that he obtains exactly what he seeks.

Some of the earliest native examples of druggists' bottles, both for show and storage, were manufactured by Henry William Stiegel at his Manheim, Pennsylvania, glasshouse. These are among the most ornate of drug bottles, with enameled flowers and foliage adorning the sides of tall rectangular containers. They typically had chamfered corners and high shoulders, much like case bottles of the period. They were free-blown by the half-post method in clear or sapphire glass and were decorated with designs in yellow, white, blue, green, and red enamel. Conventionalized floral designs are most common, but wreaths, doves, ships, parrots, roosters, birds, dogs, and cows may also appear.

Stiegel did not confine himself solely to fancy ware. He also produced vast numbers of the tiny tubular containers known as vials, used by the pharmacist to dispense most of his remedies. Between 1769 and 1770 Stiegel put 6,318 of these little bottles into stock. They are extremely simple in form, with a flared lip and open pontil, and it is difficult to distinguish Stiegel's products from similar vessels advertised by Dyott and the Boston Glass Manufactory. Vials were blown both free-hand and in molds well into the nineteenth century and are readily available to collectors. Since they were usually of aqua glass and seldom embossed, there is no great interest in them. However, you may occasionally find a doctor's medicine chest containing several dozen of them, each labeled and complete with its particular medicinal compound. These are of great historical interest and are most collectible.

During the nineteenth century, extremely attractive milk glass jars were used for storing medicines. Like the show bottles, they were considered permanent containers and were labeled with paint or gilding. A large number of such vessels was manufactured by the Millville, New Jersey, glass factory erected in 1806 by James Lee, later owned by Whitall Brothers and then by Whitall, Tatum and Company. Early examples are free-blown in an opaque white glass and fitted with a separate thin, clear glass label which is curved to follow the contour of the jar. This method of identification was patented in 1862 by William M. Walton of New York and was widely used thereafter. Traditionally, the printing on the label is in black and gold.

In the later years of the last century Whitall, Tatum produced large quantities of mold-blown milk glass jars. These lacked the vitality and charm of their free-formed predecessors, but are interesting to the collector because the name of the compound and, occasionally, the name of the apothecary are embossed on the bottles.

There were, of course, a great many other containers used in drugstores. Many of them are rather ordinary, unembossed bottles. As early as 1824 the *United States Gazette* of Philadelphia carried an advertisement by Philadelphia's Thomas Dyott enumerating some of the types available:

PHILADELPHIA AND KENSINGTON
VIAL AND BOTTLE FACTORIES IN BLAST
The subscriber having commenced the manufacturer of vials, bottles &c, on an extensive scale is enabled to supply any quantity of the following description of Apothecaries and other glasswares:
Apothecaries vials from a drachm to eight ounces.
Tincture bottles with ground stoppers, from half pint to one gallon.
Druggists' packing bottles, wide and narrow mouths, from half pint to two gallons. With every other description of vials and bottles made to order, on the most reasonable terms.

T. W. DYOTT

The so-called tincture bottles were for the most part intended to be reused. They ranged in size from a few inches to more than a foot and generally had ground-glass stoppers and ground neck interiors to assure a tight fit, rather than the usual cork closure. These vessels are also known as acid bottles because acid was often stored in them. The New England Glass Bottle Company price list of November 1, 1829, notes five different capacities for these receptacles—quart, two quart, gallon, two gallon, and three gallon. They ranged in price from thirteen cents to sixty cents each.

As mentioned in the Dyott notice, druggists' packing bottles were of two sorts, wide- and narrow-mouthed. As may be seen from those illustrated, they came in many sizes. They were, however, almost always made up in aqua or clear glass and were identified by means of paper labels. Early examples were free-blown with open pontils, while those from the last half of the nineteenth century were formed in two- or three-piece molds. Since they are rather plain, these receptacles are usually of little interest to collectors even when they bear the original labels. The labels themselves may be quite ornate, though, as

Labeled clear glass drug bottles. From the left: Podophyllin; Cincho Quinine; Oil of Winter Green.

may be seen from the Billings-Clapp label.

Prescription bottles showing the embossed name and address of a druggist are much more popular. There can be no doubt that these appeared before 1850, since the Henshaw-Ward bottle from Boston illustrated in the text bears a large pontil scar. There do not seem to be a large number of pontiled druggists' bottles of this sort, for the majority of apothecaries did not start to use personalized containers until the 1870s, when major glass manufacturers developed bottle molds in standard shapes cut to receive a slug plate bearing the name of a given druggist. This innovation was most helpful to maker and user. The glass shop could use a single mold for many customers simply by taking out one slug plate and inserting another. The apothecary, on the other hand, benefited from the savings to the manufacturer, who did not have to cut a new mold for each new account.

These individually marked drug bottles are of some interest to collectors, many of whom choose to accumulate only those associated with a given locality or, in some cases —such as the Owl Drug Company of San Francisco, California—only a single pharmacy. Embossed bottles were, of course, designed as a form of advertising; and the Owl chain used a substantial number of different containers in both clear and cobalt glass. They all bore the company name and generally its symbol, an owl perched on a mortar and clutching a pestle in one claw.

Figural embossings such as the above are relatively uncommon on drug bottles. When they do occur, they are most often forms, such as the mortar and pestle, that relate to the trade. Most bottles are round, square, or rectangular and are highly functional, with a minimum of decoration. Clear and aqua glass predominate; amber is less common, followed by the choice green and blue vessels.

Collecting these bottles presents a minimum of problems if you concentrate on

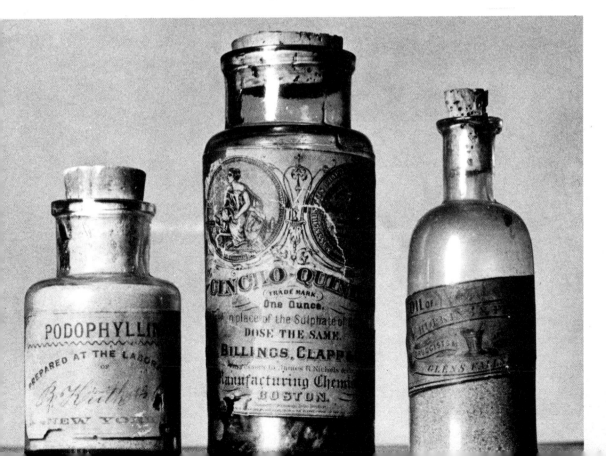

180

packing and customers' types. These are frequently encountered in bottle shops, at shows, and at dumps where they are at times the most frequently encountered forms. Window and show bottles of earlier or larger types are quite a different matter. These are sought not only by bottle collectors but also by interior decorators, who use them as planters and as decorative pieces. They are, accordingly, both expensive and hard to locate. It need hardly be said, also, that very few of the early Stiegel-type vessels are available.

It should also be noted in passing that the druggist and his mysterious potions were as much a mystery to our ancestors as to ourselves; and at times the good man felt constrained to point out to the populace that the remedies were, indeed, beneficial. As the apothecary Frederick Bull of Hartford said: "Those who think that the artickles have degenerated since the days of the ANCIENT SAMARITAN from whom this establishment took its name, are invited to call and judge for themselves.... Although the above [remedies] were selected for the sick and wounded, the healthy need not fear any ill effects from their proper use" (*Connecticut Courant,* June 28, 1823).

Opposite: Early black glass drug bottle blown in three-piece mold with painted label, "T. R. Gent Co." (Courtesy Jim Wetzel) *Above:* Aqua narrow-neck pharmacists' storage bottles.

18
Poison Bottles

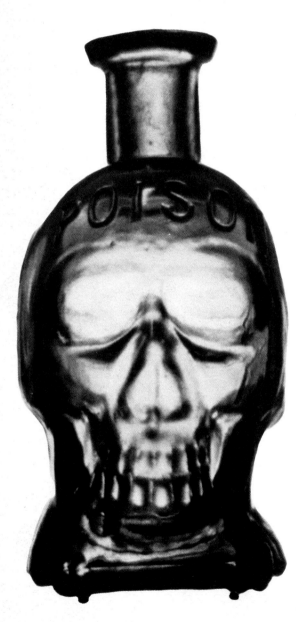

Poisons in a wide range have been used for many centuries, for purposes both beneficial and malicious. In either case it has always been necessary for the owner of the dangerous substance to identify it in some way in order to reduce the likelihood of accidental ingestion.

Various methods have been used to mark poison bottles. In Europe, nineteenth-century Danish apothecary jars containing poisons were required to be embossed or painted with three large "plus" signs, a custom still followed in many European countries. Enameled, embossed, or gilded warnings were also employed. However, since many people could not read and others might handle the containers under less than adequate lighting conditions, more positive methods were required.

At least as early as the first years of the eighteenth century, elaborate quilted bottles termed "poison flasks" appeared both in this country and in Europe. These lovely vessels are mold-blown and expanded and in most cases are made by the old Germanic half-post method. They come in a wide range of colors: purple, aqua, various shades of amber, amethyst, green, violet, blue, and yellow, among others. They are generally of a flat ovoid shape and bear a distinct resemblance to the early pocket bottles manufactured by Henry William Stiegel. The difference is that the poison bottles have a tight cross-hatch sur-

Above left: Figural poison bottle, cobalt blue skull embossed "Poison." (Courtesy Jim Wetzel)
Opposite: Poison bottles: clear glass, quilted, unmarked; formaldehyde bottle, "The Egyptian Chemical Company"; coffin-shaped, embossed "Poison, Boston, Mass." (Courtesy Jim Wetzel)

face that gives a distinctly "prickly" feel to the bottle. Almost all examples are pontiled, and they range in size from a few ounces to slightly over a pint.

There is sharp disagreement among collectors as to whether the so-called poison flasks were ever actually made in this country—and, in fact, as to whether they are even poison containers at all. At present, though, many collectors treat them as such, and due to their attractive shapes and hues, they are among the most sought-after and expensive bottles in this category.

One thing is certain. It was not until well into the nineteenth century that the dangers of mislabeled or unmarked poison receptacles gained official attention. In 1829, New York State made mandatory the requirement that the word "poison" appear on containers used for dangerous substances. Thereafter, in 1853, the American Pharmaceutical Association recommended that either the word "poison" or a death's head symbol— the familiar skull and crossbones, originally a religious sign that in the Middle Ages had come to be associated with danger and death

—or both be placed on all vessels intended for poisonous compounds.

Though some time appears to have elapsed, this suggestion was implemented eventually. There are a substantial number of poison bottles embellished with the gruesome skull and bones. Samuel Snellenberg of Philadelphia patented one of the first, a coffin-shaped receptacle embossed with the death's head, and in the same year Charles P. Booth of Atlantic City, New Jersey, obtained a governmental monopoly on a somewhat similar container. Several variations on the same theme are illustrated in this book. It is interesting to note that all bear both the symbolic sign of death and the word "poison," often repeated several times. Moreover, in several cases, raised quilting or knoblike protrusions appear on the surface of the receptacle.

The rough—and in some cases almost painfully sharp—surface thus produced appeared first in the early poison flasks and clearly seems to have been intended to alert people to the fact that what they held in their hand was not an ordinary bottle. The Whitall, Tatum glass company of Millville, New Jersey, first manufactured the later version of the quilted surface bottle in 1872, the very year that the American Medical Association suggested that druggists employ rough-textured colored glass vessels for the storage and dispensing of dangerous medicines. Whitall, Tatum became one of the leading producers in this field. Its cobalt blue cylindrical bottles were offered in nine sizes, from the seldom seen half ounce to sixteen-ounce storage bottles. In the early years of this century, the half ounce sold for $3.00 per gross and the sixteen ounce at $16.50 for the same number. An unusual rectangular glass stopper with sharp protruding edges was designed to seal these containers. Whitall, Tatum poisons were made in such great numbers that they are readily found today. This, coupled with the appealing shape and size variety available, makes them a great favorite with beginning collectors in the field.

Many other manufacturers also made quilted or knobby-surfaced poison bottles, so that they appear in various shapes and sizes as well as colors. While most are circular, triangular, or six- or eight-sided, oval ones are also known. Blue is by far the preferred hue, though various shades of amber, green, and yellow also appear. Clear and aqua glass, which appear almost exclusively in those poisons handled professionally, are the rare shades in the field of poison collecting, exactly the opposite of the situation encountered in other fields of bottle collecting.

An interesting variation frequently encountered is the use of knobs or ribbing on a coffin-shaped container, its form gloomily predictive of the fate awaiting one who fails to heed its warning. A very large cobalt blue poison in this form is a notable example, as are several smaller versions, one of them in a lovely golden amber. The coffin shape may be one of the first of the figural poisons. A patent for a plain five-sided coffin bottle was issued October 10, 1876, to one James W. Bowles of Louisville, Kentucky. Though it is uncertain whether the Bowles container ever went into production, many similar vessels were made and utilized in the drug trade.

Pure figurals, though more common in this field than some others, cannot be considered common among poisons. Perhaps best known are the expressive cobalt skulls, like the one pictured here. The first of these was patented in 1894 by Carlton H. Lee of Boston, Massachusetts. The container was made in several sizes; one is illustrated on page 182. Another rather rare receptacle, also found in cobalt glass, is molded in the

Poison bottles. From left to right: cobalt blue, embossed "The Owl Drug Co."; clear glass rat poison container; amber bottle labeled "Phenol, Poison." (Courtesy Jim Wetzel)

Rare quilted flask-type poison bottle, free-blown and pontiled. (Courtesy Jim Wetzel)

shape of a long leg bone, with cylindrical neck and flanged collar. The patent on this form was issued in 1893 to Edward M. Cone of Newark, New Jersey.

By and large, the great majority of all poison bottles were designed for use by doctors and druggists in dispensing poisonous substances to patients or customers. Druggists and manufacturers themselves were assumed to be more sophisticated, and among the trade they employed less elaborate containers. Plain circular druggists' bottles with ground-glass stoppers were used in the back rooms of apothecary shops, as were clear or aqua glass bulk containers such as the one embossed "The Egyptian Chemical Company Poison Boston, Mass.," which is shown here. Only the addition of the word "poison" distinguishes this formaldehyde bottle from any other bulk chemical bottle.

Elaborate poison bottles had a rather short life span. Few can be traced to the period before 1870, and they gradually disappeared about 1930 as physicians and manufacturers concluded that their very shapes and colors served as an attraction to children who were the most frequent victims of household poisonings. With the increasing literacy of the adult population and the decreasing use of poisons—which had been most widely employed against pests, particularly on farms—it was found best to substitute plain amber bottles with various safety closures, principally those that could be opened only by several fairly complex movements, well beyond the ability of a small child.

At the present time poison collecting is one of the most active areas in the entire field of bottle collecting. The appealing shapes and colors combined with the attraction of a fairly limited field—there are only about two hundred different American specimens—have spurred a general movement into the area.

As a result, prices are on the rise, particularly for the more unusual items such as figurals. Collectors should also remember that, beyond the previously mentioned problem of the mysterious poison flasks, there is the sticky issue of imports. There are substantial numbers of attractive English poisons on the market, which closely resemble the American bottles in size and shape but appear mostly in apple green, a color seldom encountered in the domestic product. Many poison collectors are actively seeking and accumulating these bottles, but it need hardly be said that one should buy them intentionally, not otherwise.

With the increase in collector interest many glass dealers have begun to stock poisons, and they can be obtained at shops, at shows, and through advertisements appearing or placed in bottle publications. Also, since poisons were at one time fairly common, they often show up in dumps and storage places, particularly barns and sheds where they were used to kill rodents. The small clear glass rat poison container shown here is the sort of thing one may well find on a shelf or ledge in some forgotten outbuilding. Caution should be observed in handling such finds, for their original contents may still be present.

186

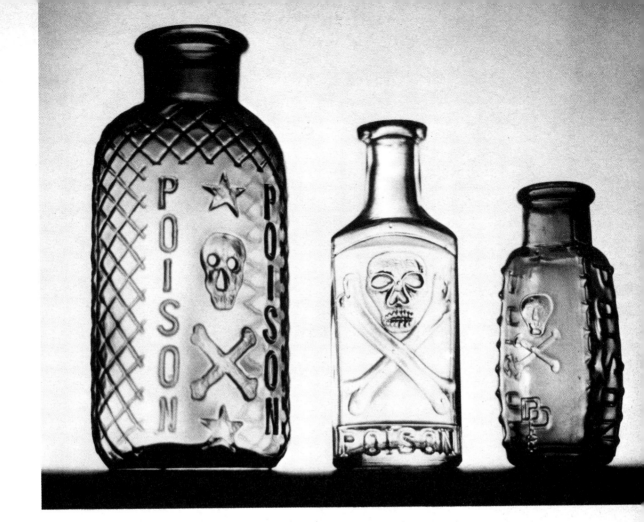

Above: Poison bottles embossed with skull, crossbones, and word "Poison." One at right is in shape of a coffin. *Left:* Poison bottles. At left, amber with raised bosses to help identify it in the dark; at right, rare triangular blue, embossed "Davis & Cick, Brooklyn." (Courtesy Jim Wetzel)

19
BARBER BOTTLES

Above: Barber bottles, matching tonic and bay rum in milk glass with painted decoration and name of owner, P. Mass. *Opposite:* Barber bottles, matching bay rum and cologne in pressed clear flint glass with ground glass stoppers. (All, courtesy Emil Walter)

In the course of the nineteenth century the barber gradually lost his quasi-medical role as healer, abandoning the letting of blood for a role more familiar to us, that of the trimmer of hair and beard. Sometime after 1850, glasshouses, particularly in Sandwich, Massachusetts, Glassboro, New Jersey, and the area around Pittsburgh, began to manufacture highly ornate bottles for the storage and dispensing of bay rum, witch hazel, cologne, and other mixtures employed by barbers. The source of such vessels was seldom marked or otherwise identified and to complicate the matter similar containers were imported from European countries during the same period. Nevertheless, barber bottles have been of great interest to collectors since at least the 1920s, a concern that is reflected in the current high prices and short supply. What draws the bottle enthusiast to these receptacles is the remarkable variety of designs and colors in which they appear.

These vessels are, in fact, a prime example of the tendency toward more elaborate types and colors that manifested itself in the last decades of the nineteenth century. As far as barber bottles were concerned, the development continued into the 1900s; some of the most interesting pieces were marketed as late as 1920, at which time the customs that justified their use were vanishing under the assault of the safety razor. The glassware of this period, variously called art or ornamental

glass, reflected a variety of technical improvements in the craft, many of which are found in barber bottles.

The earliest of these receptacles were made of pressed pattern glass in the various geometric forms developed around 1840. The batch employed was usually clear, though red, blue, and green may also appear. Pressed glass, of course, had always been thought of as a poor man's substitute for costly blown and cut vessels. In its primary phase, known as lacy glass, the sparkle and sheen associated with the more expensive product were achieved through use of intricate low-relief patterns cut into the molding press and reproduced in the ware. In 1834, the English developed fire polishing, the technique of reheating an article in order to remove tool and mold marks and to achieve a shiny surface much like that seen in the best blown and cut glass. Lacy patterns with their multitude of crevices and intricate surfaces did not lend themselves to fire polishing, so they were quickly replaced by geometric designs consisting primarily of flute, loop, diamond, and thumbprint motifs or a combination of these.

It is doubtful that barber bottles were

Barber bottles. From left to right: clear cut glass; frosted hobnail pattern glass; clear mold-blown. (Courtesy Emil Walter)

among the first examples of this new pattern glass. In fact, very few references to them are seen in nineteenth-century trade catalogs and price lists, though such a vessel does appear among the specimens of "New York Pattern Pressed Glass" illustrated in an 1868 New England Glass Company catalog. There is no doubt, however, that by the 1880s pattern glass barber bottles were extremely popular with barbers and their customers. Many of these containers were made in the shape of decanters, a form no' doubt most familiar to many of their users. The pair of pressed-glass barber bottles shown here bear etched decorative bandings and the words "Bay Rum" and "Cologne," respectively. Another illustration shows an example of frosted pattern glass, a particularly popular Victorian item in this category as well as others.

Perhaps the most interesting creation in this category was hobnail or pineapple glass, so called for the overall pattern of raised knobs or bosses covering the surface of the ware. In addition to the bottle shown here, hobnail pattern glass was blown in a number of designs and many different colors. Red, amber, yellow, blue, and green, among other hues, graced these lovely vessels. Decanters, water pitchers, sugars, and many other types appear in hobnail, but it was particularly popular with the manufacturers of barber bottles. One of the major producers in this area was Hobbs, Brockunier and Company of South Wheeling and Martin's Ferry, West Virginia. In 1886 William Leighton and William F. Russell of that company developed an opalescent hobnail made by pressing the gather of glass into the desired shape and size in specially prepared molds, then further expanding and shaping it by hand.

Until restricted by the Pure Food and Drug Act of 1906, alcohol-based substances such as bay rum and tiger rub, as well as various colognes and tonics, were made up not only by commercial sources but also by the individual barber catering to his customer's needs and preferences. The resulting invigorants were primarily used in the course of shaving or as hair tonics; and perhaps a quarter of all barber bottles bear the painted, gilded, or engraved name of such a product. The writing most often shows up on milk glass, as may be seen from the specimens illustrated in this chapter. The opaque white background was particularly suited to decoration, and it was frequently enhanced with hand-painted flowers or even scenes such as that of the millhouse and waterwheel on the hair tonic bottle shown here. Less common are the personalized containers, such as the pair marked "P. Mass." These come from a period when each regular patron of a given shop had his own set of cologne or tonics, usually two in number and, as mentioned, frequently containing mixtures made up to his order. Choicest among the personal bottles are those enhanced by a colored lithograph, usually of a reigning cabaret or stage beauty. These lithographs were pasted into a special recessed area on the side of the bottle and then covered with a clear glass panel curved to fit the contour of the bottle.

Pressed and milk glass, in one form or another, had been around for quite some time. Somewhat newer were the various forms of art glass that were also employed in the manufacture of barber bottles. These were the reflection of rapid changes in glassmaking technology during the Victorian era; and while less often seen than pressed or milk glass containers, they must have constituted a sizable percentage of the output at certain factories.

One of the most spectacular art products was Vasa Murrhina, a varicolored glass produced by dusting a gather of glass with

metallic oxides and then covering it with a second layer or coating to achieve spectacular red, brown, or blue backgrounds flecked with silver, gold, and white. The man who developed this glass was a certain Dr. Flower, the onetime proprietor of the Flower Medicine Company in Boston, Massachusetts. Flower purchased the Cape Cod Glass Works from the heirs of Deming Jarves in the early 1870s and operated it until 1882, making Vasa Murrhina barber bottles and other wares in some quantity.

Another interesting art form is striped or Lutz glass, which was a thin, transparent glass striped with colored twists. In one of the examples manufactured, white twists envelope a pale blue ground, in another type the twists or threads are also white but the background is ruby. It is not hard to see why barber bottles made in this manner were termed "candy stripers." The technique for making this glass was developed in Venice, and it was practiced at Sandwich, Massachusetts, between 1869 and 1888 under the guidance of the French glass expert Nicholas Lutz.

By far the most popular medium in which barber bottles are found is painted glass. In this country, painting or enameling on glass was known as far back as the days of Stiegel and Wistar, and it has been used, particularly for tablewares, ever since. The decoration of this sort found on barber bottles tends to the naturalistic, with bucolic motifs such as rosettes and garlands much favored. Several examples, particularly those showing the tiny dotted flower patterns associated with New Jersey shops, may be seen here. The technique was employed on both clear and colored glass. More extensive painting included full-size floral decorations featuring tulips, roses, and calla lillys as well as sea- and landscapes.

Figures also appear on some bottles. Best known among these are the picturesque creations associated with the name of Mary Gregory. Mrs. Gregory was a decorator at the Sandwich works in the last half of the nineteenth century. She specialized in quaint groups of children or young people, usually painted in white on blue, red, or green glass backgrounds. It is known that similar work was done in Central Europe and later brought into this country, and we should bear in mind that not all examples attributed to this unusual artist are necessarily from her hand. Noteworthy is a rare matching set of two barber bottles and a waste bowl. They are attributed to Mary Gregory and illustrate a quaint late-nineteenth-century tennis match. The presence of the waste bowl makes this set particularly interesting and valuable, since few of these have survived. Originally, most sets of bottles contained a waste bowl, but the bowls are large and were apparently often discarded; in any case, few survive.

Embossing on barber bottles is extremely uncommon, and makers' marks are virtually unknown. As a result it is extremely difficult to determine the origin of a given vessel, though, in some cases, such as at Sandwich, excavations on the glass factory site have uncovered fragments that allow us tentatively to attribute certain forms and types to that shop.

Bottle closures in this field are rather interesting and unusually attractive. Silver and britannia metal were used, as were porcelain tops with cork fittings. Unfortunately, many of them have been lost, so that replacements are quickly snatched up by collectors.

Color is by far the most spectacular element in the design of a barber bottle and the thing most collectors look for. Milk glass in

several variations, including pink and blue, is found, as well as red, pink, purple, amethyst, blue, yellow, green, and various shades of amber. The combination of these colors with engraving, gilding, and painting makes for one of the most visually exciting areas in the entire field of bottles.

The individual who wishes to establish a representative collection of barber bottles must be prepared to spend a substantial sum of money. As attractive as they are, these bottles were seldom discarded unless they were broken. They are not found in garbage dumps and only rarely in attics or old stores, though it never hurts to check out auctions or dispersions of the contents of old barber shops. For the most part, though, one must buy from dealers or through mail order.

20
CANDY CONTAINERS

Above: Pressed glass candy container in form of doll carriage with tin cover. *Opposite:* Candy container, clear pressed glass windmill with red tin blades. (Both, courtesy H. and B. Shatoff)

Though generally not as old as most other glass containers, candy bottles are of particular interest to many collectors. Not only do they offer a wide variety of interesting figurals, but, for many people the receptacles have a direct and pleasant association with childhood.

The first specimens of these popular bottles appeared in 1876 when a replica of Independence Hall and another of the Liberty Bell were manufactured as souvenirs to be sold to the thousands of patriotic citizens flocking to Philadelphia for the Centennial festivities. A few other examples from the nineteenth century are known, including a milk glass representation of the battleship *Maine*. (The *Maine* was blown up in Havana Harbor on February 15, 1898, and its destruction was a major factor leading to the Spanish-American War.)

It was not, however, until after 1900 that the candy container fad really caught on. The first specimens were mold-blown and hand-finished; and while a four-man team of glassblowers might produce a thousand of them in a day, they were still too expensive to justify mass production. With the development of the automatic bottle machine, however, it became possible to manufacture and sell a wide variety of glass toys at prices appealing to the general public.

The earliest of these containers were clearly designed to appeal to adults rather

than to children. The Centennial and patriotic mementos of the late 1800s were followed by political items, such as hats and small replicas of the lanterns carried in campaign processions. These receptacles, which were given out at the candidates' headquarters and along the line of march, were generally made of clear glass. They were filled with tiny multi-hued candy pellets bearing such exotic names as May Belles, Chu Chus, and Dew Drops. The sweets served to add color to the bottles and were, no doubt, an added attraction to voters.

From 1910 until well into the 1930s, candy containers were offered as keepsakes at historical sites such as Niagara Falls or Valley Forge, in countless hotels and cities, and, naturally, of momentous events, such as Lindberg's transatlantic crossing. In some cases the toy would be designed to reflect the place or event (a glass Washington's Monument or a replica of Lindy's airplane), but more often a simple paper label with the words "Souvenir of . . ." would be attached to a more common form, such as a suitcase or train engine.

While adult mementos continued to be made, the emphasis after 1930 gradually shifted to the younger generation. Simple machine-pressed toys appeared in great num-

bers. Animals, particularly rabbits, bears, and dogs, became popular, as did human figures and, of course, Santa Claus. Musical instruments, particularly horns and whistles which would blow, appeared, as well as telephones, radios, and other modern conveniences.

On the whole, there seems to have been an emphasis on masculine interests; a large number of creations were clearly designed to attract the little boy. Pistols, a variety of army tanks, automobiles, trains, and busses, as well as exotics like oil wells and steam engines, were designed for little brother. His sister had to content herself with carpet sweepers, baby bottles, and rolling pins.

The vast majority of candy containers are found in clear glass. Milk glass, while used somewhat in the late nineteenth century, was most popular between 1906 and 1912. In some cases it was combined with hand-painted details, as in a small clock that is known. This is a rare and unusual piece, particularly as the bucolic seascape is still intact. Since glass toys were painted after they had been cooled, the surface color chips or rubs off easily. Many now-colorless containers were once carefully painted. Though a painter occasionally might have decorated an entire piece, it was more common to use color as a highlight. For example, an early Victor phonograph has a black horn, but no other tinting.

While hand-colored receptacles are common and milk glass fairly so, colored glass specimens are exceedingly rare. A few were produced during the 1920s—an amber Liberty Bell and a blue fire engine are known—but they are exceedingly hard to find.

However, even if the collector is limited to clear glass, he can build a substantial and interesting collection. Nearly a thousand different forms are known and some of these are excellent figurals. For example, a radio that was made is not only a good replica of contemporary receivers but is also a very nice piece of sculptural folk art. In some areas, notably those of the automobile and airplane, one may trace the development of the vehicle in its candy bottle counterpart. Tin-roofed touring cars and Model "T"s of the twenties were replaced by the sleek vehicles of the late thirties and, finally, by the ubiquitous jeep of World War II.

This development in structure helps to date many containers, as do their accessories. The first receptacles had tin or pewter tops, and, correspondingly, in the early years of this century more metal was employed—for

Pressed glass candy containers in form of telephones with wood, metal, and string accessories. Note remnants of original candy. (Courtesy H. and B. Shatoff)

wheels, doors, propellers, and hooks. In fact, in some cases the glass was secondary, being completely surrounded by tin. Such is the case with certain cannons and lanterns of the thirties. The advent of World War II brought an end to the use of metal. Paper and cardboard wings or propellers were employed on airplanes, wooden wheels on land vehicles. By the time the war was over plastic had been developed, and it filled the role formerly occupied by tin. Thus, the nonglass portions of a container may serve to determine roughly the period in which it was produced.

The embossing that appears on candy bottles may also serve to fix a container's age. Prior to 1912 few of the receptacles were marked in any way. In that year an amendment to the Pure Food and Drug Act required that the manufacturer and packer have their names blown into the glass. Then, in the forties, it became common for the word "contents," plus a list of such, to appear embossed in the glass or printed on an attached label.

Candy bottle collecting is presently an extremely popular area of the bottle field. Early containers and those in milk or colored glass are eagerly sought and command substantial prices. Later pieces and those of less interesting form are often available at antique shops or bottle shows, but the choice receptacles are best located through advertisements in antiques and bottle periodicals. Since they were always regarded as objects to be preserved, very few candy containers will be found in old dumps or storage areas. And since many of the most attractive pieces were made in the last fifty years, it is certain that many remain in private homes. Accordingly, the enthusiast in this area may find it to his advantage to make inquiries in his community.

21
Miscellaneous Glass

Above: Clear glass insect trap embossed "Unique Fly Trap," tin screw top. (Courtesy Staten Island Historical Society) *Opposite top:* Lithographed tin carrying box for the Shur-Stop Fire Extinguisher. *Opposite bottom:* Same box open to show red painted glass fire extinguisher bottles or balls. (Courtesy Helene and Barry Shatoff)

Bottle collectors have chosen to include within the ambit of their hobby several groups or types of glass objects which for the most part are neither bottles nor even bottle-shaped. They are, however, both interesting and of great interest to collectors.

Many of these devices are ball-shaped, among the most unusual and attractive of which are the so-called witch balls. At least as early as the seventeenth century, glassmakers, who were generally a superstitious and uneducated lot, were blowing hollow glass balls, which by custom were hung in fireplace chimneys, windows, and doors to prevent the entrance of witches and other evil spirits. To what extent these globes were really believed to have talismanic powers (as opposed to their decorative function) is unclear, but there is evidence that as late as the middle of the last century they were being used to ward off ill luck. A brief passage in Samuel Hopkins Adams's *Grandfather Stories* makes reference to the fact that flatboat crews on the Erie Canal commonly decked their craft with hex brooms and "witch balls; blue, green and amber, moulded at the Mt. Vernon Glass Factory, in the Oneida hills." Some credence is given to this story by the fact that there exists at least one of these globes which was blown in a three-piece mold known to have been utilized at the Mount Vernon shop. While there are a few other mold-formed pieces, including one in

sapphire blue which was shaped in a Keene, New Hampshire, pint decanter mold, and another whose design may be traced to an inkwell mold, most witch balls were free-blown.

The manufacture of these objects seems to have been rather widespread throughout nineteenth-century American glasshouses. McKearin's *American Glass* makes reference to examples traceable to factories at Cleveland, Mount Vernon, and Ellenville, New York; Millville, New Jersey; and Keene, New Hampshire.

The association of many of the globes with tall vaselike objects, traditionally termed witch-ball holders, gives credence to the belief that, in later years at least, they were primarily intended to be decorative parlor objects. The globes were also employed as covers for wide-mouth jars and quite possibly were the forerunners of today's Christmas tree balls. One authority speculates that the custom of hanging varicolored witch balls in windows led eventually to their being suspended from the arms of candletrows. The latter were wooden, treelike framworks popular in Europe in the late Middle Ages at Christmas. From this it was a simple progression to lighter-weight balls suitable for hanging in the branches of a yule tree.

There is no doubt that by 1871 Christmas tree balls were being produced commercially in large quantities. In that year William A. Demuth of New York City advertised himself in the City Directory as a "Manufacturer of silvered glass balls for the Christmas Tree, in all colors and sizes." The Louisville Glass Works, active at Louisville, Kentucky, ca. 1855–1873, also made such balls in amber and cobalt as well as in aquamarine streaked with white. There were no doubt many other makers, but little is presently known of their efforts. Interestingly enough,

though, collectors are now beginning to turn their attention to the early blown tree ornaments, and it is possible that a full area of collecting may soon develop.

Witch balls are usually from two to seven inches in diameter and are found in a number of colors, including black, green, amber, blue, red, yellow, and aqua. A few rare examples from South Jersey are made of looped glass, created by embedding loops, usually of white glass, in a contrasting base. Early specimens also had silvered interiors, which was apparently due to a belief that this improved their capacities to ward off witches. Since these spheres usually contained a hole where the blow pipe was broken off, they were often plugged with a cork or wooden peg and used as containers.

A direct descendant of the witchball is the target ball. These were small globes used in target shooting by nineteenth-century sportsmen. The practice of shooting at moving targets, live or otherwise, has always been popular in this country. Initially, pigeons were employed; the birds were released from small traps and marksmen would try to bring them down with rifles or shot guns. Certain public resentment of the sport, coupled with problems in raising, transporting, and releasing the birds, led the shooters to seek a more efficient method. English sportsmen in the 1830s devised the idea of employing blown glass balls, filled with smoke, confetti, silk ribbon, or feathers to more clearly mark the shot when broken. Charles Portlock of Boston, Massachusetts, introduced such devices to this country in the mid 1850s, but they obtained real popularity through the efforts of Buffalo Bill Cody and his sidekick Annie Oakley. These thespians would astound large crowds by shooting a half dozen balls out of the air at one time. Of course they hedged their bets a bit by utilizing large caliber

Pressed glass lightning rod balls. At left,
blue milk glass; at right, white milk glass.
(Courtesy Helene and Barry Shatoff)

pistols with shot shells containing fine bird shot. Since even a single pellet would shatter the fragile "birds," anything in the general vicinity would suffice.

At first target balls were thrown into the air by hand, but in the 1880s Captain Adam Bogardus perfected a mechanical throwing device. This, being a more predictable and convenient method, greatly increased interest in the sport. Bogardus also, as one might expect, manufactured target balls, one of the more sought-after types being embossed "Bogardus Glass Ball Pat'd Apr 10 1877."

The earliest balls were simple glass spheres, but by 1860 blown molded specimens with decorative embossings began to appear. At first these were simply raised ribbings or diamond-shaped patterns intended to decrease the likelihood of the shot glancing off the smooth surface without shattering the ball. It was not long, though, before enterprising manufacturers and tradesmen realized that the globes provided an excellent advertising medium. Without doubt one of the most elaborate examples of this is the amber glass ball made in Pittsburgh, which was embossed "From JH Johnston/Great Western Gun Works/164 Smithfield Street/Pittsburgh, Pa./Rifles, Shot Guns/Revolvers, Ammunition/Fishing Tackle/Choke Boring Repairing/&/Write for Price List." All of that on a three-inch disposable globe! Other balls bear different advertisements and, in some cases, embossed figures of dogs, hunters, and the like.

It is extremely difficult to determine the origin of most target balls. Glass company price lists seldom allude to them, and most advertising was that of suppliers. There is, though, a rare aquamarine specimen marked "Manufactured by the/Kentucky Glass Works Company/Joseph Griffith & Sons Sole

Agents/also Dealers in Guns, Pistols and Fishing Tackle, Louisville/Kentucky." It was made at the Kentucky Glass Works in Louisville between 1880 and 1890.

Target balls are not common. They were produced for little more than thirty years; the latest known patent mark is 1893. Their demise had been signaled thirteen years earlier by George Ligowsky's invention of the clay pigeon, a flat clay disk that provided a less fragile and more economical target. Moreover, since they were designed to be destroyed, there was little incentive to preserve them. A few have survived though, quite possibly due to the unusual embossments and rather wide range of color, including aqua, green, cobalt, amber, amethyst, and clear.

Very similar in form to target and witch balls are fishermen's floats or toggle balls. These, however, come in a much greater size range, some being as large as a foot in diameter. These globes, which were intended to mark or hold up the edges of large fishing nets, have been made throughout the world, including here in the United States. American examples are not marked, so it is most difficult to say when or where they were made. The nature of their use reduces the likelihood of long survival for these vessels, and most do not date before 1900. It should be noted that Japanese floats made as late as the 1940s bear pontil marks and signs of hand blowing, thus creating the impression that they were made much earlier than they really were.

While their use is declining, toggle balls are still used by some fishermen, particularly the Japanese. They are also being imported for use as decorator and souvenir items. Most are found in some shade of green or aqua, though red, amber, and amethyst may also be seen.

Most popular of all these vessels as far as collectors are concerned are fire extinguisher bottles. And they are available in the most notable variety. Unlike the items previously discussed, these are true bottles in the sense that they were intended to hold a fluid, in this case carbon tetrachloride. As early as 1820 large carboys of acid were carried to fires, where the firemen would pour soda into them to produce a fire extinguishing mixture which was then propelled through the hose and onto the flames by the force of its own chemical reaction.

Sometime after 1850 much smaller containers for fire-smothering fluids began to appear on the market. The first extinguisher patent was issued in 1863 to one Alanson Crane of Fortress Monroe, Virginia, but there is little doubt that the devices antedate this period. Primitive examples were probably simple glass spheres filled with extinguishing fluid, which were to be thrown on a fire when needed. Upon shattering they produced a nonflammable foam. As late as 1910 the International Fire Equipment company of West New Brighton, New York, was manufacturing such globes. The set pic-

tured came in a metal box with the enameled advice "Throw Extinguisher at base of flame." The balls were painted a bright red and stored in the carrier by means of wire clips. The International Fire Equipment Corporation also produced an automatic fire extinguisher. This device, the Shur-Stop, consisted of a single bulblike receptacle suspended in a wire rack. At 130°F, the solder holding the bulb in its rack would melt, allowing the extinguisher bottle to fall into the fire.

If all extinguisher bottles were as plain as the Shur-Stop products, collectors would not be likely to show much interest in them. Happily, however, most makers showed a decided preference for attractive colors in their products, and a surprising number employed unusual shapes as well. One of the most bizarre and lovely is the cobalt blue Rockford Kalamazoo Automatic and Hand Fire Extinguisher. It is eleven inches tall and made in the form of a kerosene lamp chimney. Another unusual type was the barrel-shaped amber Hazelton's High Pressure Chemical Fire Keg. Both these figurals date from around 1890, and both are much sought after by collectors.

Earlier bottles were fairly standard in form, being a heavy glass globe surmounted by a long neck. Most such extinguishers were embossed with the name of the manufacturer and most were available in sets, usually of three, which were transported and stored in wire carriers.

There were two major producers of these standard form fire extinguisher bottles, the Harden Hand Fire Extinguisher Company of Chicago, Illinois, and the Hayward Company of New York City. The former had patented its first device in 1871. Harden globes were blown in two molds, one with vertical ribs, the other with a quilted surface. In either case a star appears on one side of the bottle and the words "Harden s Hand Fire Extinguisher" appear on a band running around the middle of the vessel. These bottles are found in emerald green, cobalt, and teal.

Hayward products, interestingly enough, were also patented for the first time in 1871 and, like their major competitor, received wide distribution throughout this and other countries. The form of the Hayward bottle is similar to that produced by Harden. The surface is covered with a series of raised diamond-shaped panels, upon one of which appears the monogram HNS. A large number of colors are known, including green, blue, smoke, and amber. A second and somewhat different product, Hayward's Hand Grenade Fire Extinguisher, was made only in blue glass.

All other types of fire extinguisher bottles are much less common than those made by the two major sources. Among the rarest and most interesting are milk glass grenades with heavily embossed floral patterns covering most of the surfaces. Some people have mistaken these bottles for colognes, but the existence of specimens complete with contents should relieve all doubts on this point. An identical clear glass version of this bottle is also known.

Perhaps the most unusual of all these receptacles is the Little Giant Fire Extinguisher, a rare explosive grenade containing a large firecracker set into the globe. The theory was that the flames would ignite the firecracker fuse, causing an explosion which would, in turn, shatter the glass and discharge the contents onto the conflagration. This, like the Shur-Stop Automatic Fireman, was an attempt to solve the problem of fires in unattended buildings, a situation now resolved through the use of automatic sprinkler systems.

Since extinguisher bottles, like target balls, were made only to be destroyed, they are in relatively short supply. A surprising quantity has been uncovered, however, many of them from old buildings where they have remained in place for decades. Often such vessels still retain their wax- or cement-sealed cork closures and the contents are still in place, a condition which greatly enhances their value to serious collectors.

In the past five years bottle buffs have also shown increasing interest in lightning rod balls as a field for exploration. These globe- or sphere-shaped forms were made in great numbers during the late nineteenth and early twentieth centuries as decorative items to be placed on the lightning rods that graced most barn and farmhouse roofs. They are a distinctly rural phenomenon, and large numbers may still be seen high on barn roofs all the way from New York to Wisconsin. Typically, a single ball is set on each rod about a third of the way up from the rooftop. In some cases as many as three globes may appear on a single rod.

As may be seen from the examples illustrated, milk glass is most popular in this field. Blue and white milk glass is found in a multitude of shapes and patterns. Some pieces are just plain globes. Others are ribbed or embossed or impressed with sunbursts, crescents, and stars. Ribs and fluting appear as well as diamond patterning. The multitude and diversity of such decoration seems odd, since the objects normally are placed so far from the ground it is difficult for the designs to be seen. Solid colored balls in red, blue, amethyst, green, and amber are relatively common. Often a patriotic motif is discerned, with three balls—red, white, and blue—ranged across the rooftop.

Very little is known about the origin of these objects. They are seldom mentioned in glasshouse inventories, and while trade names such as "Electra" appear on some examples, little research has yet been undertaken as to patent dates and manufacturers. The range of shapes and colors, however, makes the area one that should attract further collectors.

Shown here, also, is a specimen of another bottle type which has shown some appeal. It is embossed "Unique Fly Trap," a rather exact definition of its purpose. Flies and other winged insects have long been regarded as both a nuisance about the house and a potential source of disease. In early America a bulbous decanter form was used as an efficient trap for these pests. The vessel, like the one shown, had an open bottom that stood clear of the surface on three ball feet. The lower rim curled upward and inward, providing a narrow trough into which beer or ale was poured. As it soured, this liquid proved most attractive to the flying creatures, who then climbed or flew into the bottle in search of food. There they were rendered unconscious by the strong fumes, falling into the trough and drowning.

The earliest American examples of this form date from the 1860s and are distinctly like decanters in shape. They are either free-formed or blown in three-piece molds. Later specimens, like the one illustrated, are constructed more scientifically, containing screens to prevent escape and wide mouths with screw-top covers for ease in cleaning.

Since only a limited number of types are known, fly traps cannot be regarded as a major collecting area. They are, however, often combined by collectors with accumulations of mouse and rat traps or similar devices.

The ease with which you can obtain a representative grouping of any of these more esoteric glass objects depends to a great extent on what you are collecting. Lightning rod balls are abundant, more so perhaps on barns than in shops, but anyone who wants a few can find them. Witch balls and fishermen's floats are seemingly in good supply, but only because there are so many imported examples around. Old mold-blown American witch balls are extremely rare, free-blown examples only slightly less so. Target balls, particularly embossed ones, are also hard to get. Fire extinguisher bottles are in great demand at present, but for a price one may assemble a fair grouping of the more common types. These may also on occasion be located in old buildings and storage areas. Advertisements in bottle publications should locate samples of all of these as well as fly traps, of which, as mentioned, there are not too many variants.

Opposite: Amber Hazelton's High Pressure Fire Keg, an unusual form similar to shapes found in whiskey and bitters bottles. *Above:* Hayward fire extinguisher bottle, with raised diamond-shaped panels and monogram "HNS."

22
Bottle Collecting

Excavating bottles. The glass is handled carefully to avoid breakage.

Collecting attractive or historic bottles as a hobby or pastime is a relatively recent phenomenon. Early American hollow ware—pitchers, bowls, sugars, and other dishes—has been collected since before 1900. Until recently, though, little attention was paid to common utilitarian glass, particularly bottles.

Large numbers of these containers have survived, however, and without the aid of hobbyists. There are several reasons why. First, for many years empty bottles were of economic value. They might be used in the home as canning or storage containers, turned in at the store for a few cents, or sold in bulk to scrap dealers, who in turn delivered them to glass manufactories for use as cullet. Also, bottles are surprisingly durable, and vast numbers that were thrown on dumps or into ponds or lakes, or buried in the ground, have emerged relatively unscathed after their long confinement. The abundance of these vessels is one of the main reasons the hobby has flourished. The number of collections in many fields—such as fine furniture or early silver—is limited by the small volume of objects available. In contrast, the many thousands of bottles in circulation have enabled a much larger group to take part in this hobby.

Collecting as it is thought of today was preceded by a long period in which people preserved certain bottles simply because they were attractive, at a time when few decorative items were available to the average house-

Bottles are found in unusual places, such as beneath the foundations of old buildings.

holder. Figured flasks and figural bottles were produced in large numbers, and a substantial percentage of them were preserved simply because they looked pretty. Early bottle collectors such as John Spargo, Stephen Van Rensselaer, and George S. McKearin made regular buying trips through rural areas, where they found vast numbers of bottles resting in places of honor on mantels or table tops or carefully stored away in trunks. The owners of these receptacles in most cases had little knowledge of their origin and showed no interest in such details as maker's name, mode of design, or purpose. They were content with the object itself.

The modern collector is largely distinguished from such predecessors by a desire not only to accumulate substantial numbers of bottles but also to learn something about them and about those who made them.

This interest was first expressed in 1900, when Edwin Atlee Barber, a pioneer glass and pottery expert, wrote *American Glassware*. This was followed in 1921 by Stephen Van Rensselaer's *Early American Bottles and Flasks*. By the 1920s the relatively few serious collectors had begun to realize that they were dealing with a vast area and that within the broad field there were various categories worthy of individual attention. In *Early American Bottles* and its 1926 revision, Van Rensselaer attempted for the first time to sort out one of these areas, figural flasks. He established a system of classification by type and subject matter, which was widely accepted until it was supplanted in 1941 by a more complete and rational system, devised by George S. and Helen McKearin, authors of *American Glass*.

These books reflected the growing interest in bottles, though they were almost entirely confined to earlier, more valuable types; furthermore, through their circulation among antiques buffs, they provided an impetus for the hobby. By the beginning of the Second World War there were probably several thousand serious collectors scattered across the United States. They were interested mostly in flasks, early black glass, bitters, and figural bottles; and what little communication existed among them was fostered by dealers like McKearin, who regularly stocked and advertised old bottles. McKearin's and Van Rensselaer's advertisements in *Antiques Magazine* during the thirties and forties were a major stimulus to the field, as were the occasional articles by Lura Watkins and other authorities in the area.

Research, however, was limited almost exclusively to the historical background of various factories, and most collectors had only the vaguest idea of how the containers were actually made.

In the early 1950s a combination of factors led to a rapid increase in the number of bottle collections. More leisure time as well as more money for recreation led many people who had previously been uninterested in hobbies to begin to seek out such pastimes. Much of this activity took place outdoors, and the hobbyists soon found themselves exploring ghost towns, dumps, and old houses, particularly on the West Coast. They began to gather all sorts of old objects—among which were bottles, in a wide variety.

Since few of the newly discovered containers were the flasks and fine glass discussed in the few books then available, the new enthusiasts found it necessary to do their own research and establish their own categories. Antiques magazines that had come onto the market in the postwar period, such as *Spinning Wheel* and *Antiques Journal,* directed their attention to the new fields of interest; they offered articles on bitters, proprietary medicines, inks, and other bottles that had never been of interest to the established publications.

The demand for information soon became so great that nearly two hundred books dealing with various areas of bottle collecting have been published. The vast majority of these works have been privately printed by the authors themselves or by the so-called vanity press. While they vary greatly in quality, they provide an extremely important body of source material on nearly every area of the hobby.

As the number of bottle enthusiasts increased, it became evident that exchange of information and shared interests required something beyond books and magazine articles. The void was filled with a formal organization, the bottle club. In 1959 a small group of collectors in Sacramento, California, founded the Antique Bottle Collectors Association (ABA), the first of many organizations devoted to research and propagation of the bottle collectors' interests. (Though ABA has now passed from the scene, discontinuing its activities early in 1974, there are numerous local groups, each serving a given area or specialty. While there is no central listing of these organizations, an interested collector will have no trouble learning of a club in his area if he makes inquiries among his fellow enthusiasts.)

The high point of such activity seems to have been the late 1960s, and at present there seems to be a decline of interest; more serious collectors are becoming dissatisfied with the general interest club, which often functions mostly as a social organization. Some of these clubs are now disbanding, but they are often replaced with specialized organizations devoted to a specific area, such as fruit jars or figurals, and offering more in-depth material on the field in question. The club newsletters put out by such bodies often are of a high quality and contain examples of original research, providing a real addition to the body of material available.

It should not be assumed, however, that the occasional disbanding of a bottle club, or declining prices in the bottle market, indicate a general decrease in interest on the part of hobbyists. Quite the contrary. Today, bottle collecting is the second leading American hobby, with several million enthusiastic followers, and there is no reason to believe that this interest will wane. The bottles are there by the thousands, their form, color, and history a constant challenge to the collector. As more is learned in each category about the containers and their antecedents, more people will be enticed into starting collections. And despite price increases in certain areas, the cost of this hobby remains remarkably low in comparison to most others. This is particularly important in attracting young hobbyists, who can continue to enter the field in large numbers as long as old dumps and cellars remain to provide them with inexpensive sources for their collections.

Any hobby reflects the personality of the individual, and bottle collecting is no exception. Accordingly, we cannot lay down any hard and fast rules for the beginning collector, but we can offer some general guidelines that will help you in forming your collection.

First, bottle collecting today is a highly competitive enterprise. In every desirable area, the choice vessels are in great demand, and the supply is limited. Such seemingly mundane objects as fruit jars and medicine bottles may sell for thousands of dollars each, even though esthetically they cannot be compared with a fine flask or figural bottle. It is obvious that if only a half-dozen specimens of a given container are known, only a half-dozen—or fewer—collectors can own them. The collector must therefore set reasonable limits on his ambitions. Nothing is as likely to lead to frustration as the attempt to obtain all the fascinating or beautiful specimens that exist. You cannot own everything.

Limited collections generally prove to be the most interesting and successful in the long run. Try to organize your collection around a specific theme, such as color, a specific glassmaker, local history, or a particular bottle type. A concentrated area, too, is easier to research—for the true collector inevitably becomes as interested in the history of his artifacts as in the objects themselves. Moreover, because of their general resemblance in shape and color, most bottles tend to become boring when viewed in large numbers. A collection of several hundred vessels is unwieldy and difficult to display effectively. The better rule is to prune efficiently, to reduce the number of common or damaged bottles in a collection when better examples are acquired. You can then sell or trade the discarded examples and so obtain the means to acquire more desirable pieces.

This leads to a second general recommendation. Always try to acquire the best specimens you can afford. Since most collectors buy (rather than find) most of their bottles, cost is a major consideration. When faced with a choice, the beginner often tends to buy five one-dollar bottles rather than a single bottle for five dollars. Assuming that the vessels are fairly priced in terms of the market, this decision will almost always prove to be a poor one. Quality is what you are aiming for, not quantity. The more expensive bottle is not expensive by accident. Its price reflects demand; and the demand is based on rarity or beauty, characteristics generally lacking in the cheaper items. So buy the best you can afford. You can be sure

that really good bottles will not only be a continuing source of pleasure but will increase in value over the years, while the common items will not.

When you are deciding on your specific area of interest, check the comments at the end of each chapter in this book; they are designed to help you evaluate the wisdom of entering a given field. Now the process of acquisition begins. Most areas of the country today have dealers who specialize in old bottles and whose advertisements may be found in local newspapers. They are generally honest and knowledgeable people, who will not only sell what they have in stock but also will actively search for the particular vessels a collector wants. Let the dealers know what you want, and they will try to find it. Since a dealer usually has a large number of contacts, it pays to be in touch with several dealers, locally and even nationally. The various antiques magazines and newspapers, such as *Hobbies, Spinning Wheel, Antiques Journal,* and *The Antiques Trader,* are also most helpful in this regard; they carry advertisements of bottles for sale, and you can place your own ads in them for the items you are seeking.

Of course, it is possible to discover bottles yourself in various places where they have been discarded over the years—dumps, old barns, stores, cellars, and attics. "Digging" may be the most fun part of bottle collecting —if not the most immediately successful. Locality has a great deal to do with success here. Try hunting in rural areas, where life is more stable and where bottles may have remained right where they are for years— and where fewer collectors have had a chance to discover sources. Take a walk through the woods or through overgrown farmland; you may well stumble on an abandoned dump, with a horde of objects deposited in years gone by when the place was still inhabited. Investigate out-of-the way places. The land around a "No Dumping" sign, for instance, may indicate that people once did dump their trash—and bottles—there; it may well contain the things you're looking for. Check out local garage sales; even the tiniest will contain bottles. Old country houses up for sale are sometimes good sources; their former inhabitants may have abandoned bottles they thought were worthless.

On a larger scope, the Eastern seaboard, which has some of the oldest settlements in the country, can provide some of the oldest bottles. It is here that black glass wines, open pontiled medicines, and rare flasks are most likely to come to light. Possibilities are particularly bright today in the Southeastern coastal states. Collector interest developed there at a later date, and destructive frosts and ground freezes have not affected buried glass as they have in the North. Western states cannot usually boast of the production of such ancient bottles, but they have, particularly in desert areas, an abundance of the lovely sun-colored glass so dear to collectors' hearts. Moreover, there, as in the South, a milder climate has tended to preserve discarded containers.

In all areas, lakes, rivers, and canals may yield choice specimens preserved for decades beneath the waters. Many of these will show the chalky white or iridescent discoloration, termed "sickness," that reflects the decomposition of the glass in a moist environment.

However and wherever you may obtain the nucleus of your collection, it is good practice to develop the habit of cataloging the pieces. Mark the individual bottles in an inconspicuous place with a numerical or alphabetical code, and key the code to a book in which you record, for each bottle, informa-

tion on its source, cost or other index of value, and historical background. This is obviously important if you want to resell or trade the specimen, and is at least equally valuable for insurance purposes. It should be noted that, with costs what they are today, many hobbyists find it necessary to insure their collections. Photographing the bottles is also important both for historical and insurance purposes.

And, of course, any collection worth having is worth storing and displaying in an attractive manner. Far too many bottles are tucked away in boxes or unattractive cabinets. More and more collectors are displaying their choice specimens on sets of wooden or glass shelves. These are bolted securely to a wall or across a window so as to take advantage of natural light. If a window is not available, artificial lighting from the back may be employed to show the glass off to its fullest beauty. It is generally desirable, also, to have shelves fronted by glass doors, as animals and children could damage or break the bottles. More and more today, too, theft is a serious problem, particularly for collectors whose specialties include the rarer and more expensive vessels, so this should be considered in any decision on how to display them.

Extra bottles, or those which the owner does not wish to have out, should always be stored in a warm, dry place. Cartons such as those used by liquor dealers, which have several separate sections, are ideal for storage and shipment of bottles. One bottle should be placed in each compartment, after having been carefully wrapped in cloth or crumpled paper.

Cleaning and repairing bottles are matters of great concern to the collector. As to the former, warm water and detergent applied with a baby bottle brush, which can be found in any drugstore, will often do the trick. For tougher stains, soaking in a bleach solution or swirling a mild abrasive (such as sand) in water around in the interior will often result in a shiny bottle. Repairing, on the other hand, is a difficult job if it is to be done correctly, and the best thing to do is to consult one of the several books on the market dealing with this field. Also, there are various people who specialize in such repairs and their addresses often appear in local telephone directories and newspaper advertisements.

Finally, a collector should learn as much as possible about the historical background of his bottles. A large number of books on antique bottles is now available, including both general texts and those concentrating on a particular specialty, such as bitters or fruit jars. But you will eventually find that books are not enough. Once you get involved you'll quickly discover how much there is still to be learned. This offers you the opportunity for original research in local libraries, using old newspapers, business directories, census records, and the like. You may find this a fascinating and rewarding enterprise, in which you'll learn more not only about your collection but also about the people and times that produced the bottles. You may even end up contributing to the general field of knowledge as well.

All of this—gathering, cataloging, and learning—goes to make up the exciting hobby of bottle collecting. To an outsider it might appear tedious and time consuming, but its position as one of the major American pastimes testifies to the fact that the hobby is alive and well in the United States and is likely to remain so.

Glossary of Glassmaking Terms

Acid-etched: A decorative technique whereby hydrofluoric acid and ammonium fluoride are employed to eat away the glass surface in decorative patterns.

Agate glass: A striated off-brown and white decorative glass made from a mix incorporating blast furnace slag.

Amberina: A type of glassware shaded in color from dark to light, typically from deep red to pale amber. It was created at the New England Glass Company in the 1830s.

Annealing: The process in which new glass is gradually cooled to room temperature in an oven or lehr.

Batch: A term applied to the mixture of raw glassmaking ingredients when they are ready for the process of melting.

Battledore: A flat shovel-shaped wooden paddle used to flatten parts of a bottle as it is being hand-formed.

Blob top: Heavy knoblike glass top designed to support closure on mineral or soda water bottles.

Block: A wooden form hollowed out on one side, used in the process of blowing glass to give symmetrical form to a bottle.

Blowpipe: A hollow iron tube, two to six feet long, used in glassblowing. The worker blows through this pipe to expand a gather of glass.

Bohemian glass: Colored, engraved, and cut glass made in the area that is now Czechoslovakia and imported into this country after 1820.

Burmese glass: A form of art glass characterized by shading from rose-pink to pale yellow. It was made primarily at the Mount Washington Glass Company in New Bedford, Massachusetts, around 1860.

Cameo glass: A form of overlay or stratified glass, generally with white or pale opaque glass superimposed on a darker base and then cut in cameo.

Clapper: A tool used by glassmakers in shaping and forming objects, particularly footings.

Closure: A device, such as a cork, cap, or stopper, used to seal a bottle or decanter.

Crown cork: Modern metal cap with cork liner used on soda and beer bottles.

Cullet: Cleaned broken glass fragments used in the glass mixture or batch to promote fusion of the materials.

Custard glass: A variant of opaque white (milk) glass in which the color is a pale off-yellow.

Cut glass: Glass decorated by incising the surface with iron or stone wheels, then finishing on a wooden wheel.

Decolorizing: The process of removing the discoloration in glass produced by iron and other impurities, through addition of manganese, arsenic, or selenium to the batch.

Dip mold: A one-piece part mold open at the top to facilitate removal of the expanded gather of glass.

Empontilling: The process of attaching a metal rod to the bottom of a bottle or other glass object to hold it while finishing the upper portion of the piece.

Enameling: Decoration of a bottle by painting it with low-temperature, vitrifiable enamels and then refiring it to fix the color.

Engraving: Decoration of glass by cutting with copper cutting wheels and diamond-point tools.

Etching: See *Acid-etched.*

Finish: The last step in the creation of a bottle—formation of the neck and lip.

Fire polishing: Reheating a finished bottle or glass object to remove tool marks and to obtain a smooth surface.

Flashing: Dipping white or clear glass in a batch of colored glass to coat it. Also known as *plating.*

Flint glass: A variety of soft, readily cut glass made from a batch containing calcined flint stone.

Fluting: Ridgelike, rounded vertical lines impressed by a mold on blown glassware.

Flux: A material such as soda that causes fusion in glassmaking.

Free-blown: Glass formed by blowing and hand and tool manipulation alone, without the aid of molds.

Frit: Glassmaking material produced by heating sand or calcined flints in a furnace.

Full mold: A mold that produces a full-size object that need not be further expanded upon removal from the mold.

Gall: A scum containing impurities, which rises to the surface of a melted batch of glass during heating. It must be removed to insure a good quality of glass.

Gather: A blob of hot glass collected on the end of the blowpipe and then expanded by blowing, to form the glass object.

Gilding: A method of decorating glass by painting brown oxide of gold on the object's surface, then refiring it.

Glassblower's chair: A workbench with long arms and extended seat specially designed for a glassblower to use in his work.

Glass pot: A clay pot or crucible in which the glass mixture or batch is melted.

Glass soap: Black oxide of manganese employed to decolorize glass.

Glory hole: An annealing oven or reheating furnace used to reheat objects as they cool during the process of shaping and fire polishing.

Green glass: Common bottle glass made from a mixture of sand, soda or potash, and lime. It was customarily green or aqua due to impurities in the batch.

Half post: A method of bottle making in which the partially blown vessel is dipped again into the molten glass, then finally expanded.

Hand-blown: Glass formed by blowing and manipulation, with the use of molds but without employment of an automatic bottle-making machine.

Insufflated: A collector's term denoting blown molded glassware.

Lehr: An annealing oven used to cool finished glass gradually.

Lead glass: A soft, readily cut glass made from a mixture of lead oxide, sand, and potash.

Lime glass: Glass made from a mixture of bicarbonate of soda, chalk (lime), sand, and niter.

Lipper: A wooden tool used to widen mouths and form the rims and spouts of jars and pitchers.

Marver: A metal or polished stone slab upon which the blower rolls and shapes his parison while blowing.

Metal: A glassblower's term for glass in either the molten or finished state.

Mold: A metal, ceramic, or wooden form with an interior design in which a gather of glass was expanded to give it shape and/or decoration.

Mold marks: Raised lines or ridges left on the body of a piece of mold-blown glass. The marks are created when the hot glass is forced out the interstices between parts of the mold by the pressure of blowing.

Mold-blown: Glass formed in whole or in part by the use of molds.

Muffle: A small furnace used in glassmaking.

Overlay: A method of decorating glass by applying several layers of metal, often in different colors, then cutting through one or more layers to provide a contrast in hues.

Offhand pieces: Glass objects, usually free-blown, made by the glassblowers in their spare time and from leftover glass. Such objects were often given as gifts to relatives and friends.

Opal glass: A dense white glass generally pressed in an overall floral or banded and ribbed pattern.

Parison: An inflated gather of molten glass.

Pattern mold: A mold, generally of the dip variety, with a decorative design cut into its interior.

Plate mold: A full-size mold, usually for bottles, with slots cut into one side so as to receive a variety of different plates, each containing the name of a different merchant.

Pontil: A long metal rod, solid or hollow, used to hold a glass object while the upper area of the object was being finished.

Pontil scar: The scar, generally of rough glass and generally circular, left on the finished bottle after removal of the pontil.

Pressed glass: Glass objects made by pressing gobs of molten glass in a mechanical mold, which is activated by a plunger or piston.

Pucellas: A metal tool used by glassmakers to shape glass. It looks somewhat like a pair of tongs or shears.

Ribbing: Protruding ridges on glass objects produced either by use of molds or by tooling.

Seam: A mold mark on a bottle. See *Mold marks.*

Sheared neck: Bottle neck cut off by shears while still in soft, hot state.

Sick glass: A collector's term denoting glass whose surface has corroded through long exposure to moisture.

Snap case: A spring-loaded cradlelike device that replaced the pontil around 1850 as a device to hold bottles while they were being finished.

Stained glass: Glass that has been colored by the application of metallic oxides.

Sun-colored glass: A collector's term for glass containing manganese (originally employed in the batch as a decolorizer) that over the years has reacted to the effect of the sun's ultraviolet rays by turning amethyst or even purple.

Three-piece mold: A common nineteenth-century mold made in three separate parts, which are hinged together to allow the expanded parison to be removed.

Tooled glass: Any blown-glass object formed or decorated through the use of glassblower's implements.

Turn mold: A term referring to the process in which bottles were spun in a greased mold to polish them and to remove mold marks.

Vasa Murrhina: A type of varicolored art glass. It was made by dusting a gather of glass with metallic oxides, which fused to the glass, then covering this with a second gather of clear metal.

Wetting off: Marking the neck of a bottle with a ring of water, so that it can be easily broken away from the blowpipe to which it was affixed during the process of expansion.

Whittle marks: Rough marks of a dimpled or wavy nature on the surface of a hand-blown bottle. These are caused by blowing the bottle in a mold that has not been properly warmed.

Index

Figures in italics refer to pages on which illustrations appear.